C000023397

Trade Secrets

Powerful Strategies for Volatile Markets

Adrian Manz

HARRIMAN HOUSE LTD

3A Penns Road
Petersfield
Hampshire
GU32 2EW
GREAT BRITAIN

Tel: +44 (0)1730 233870
Email: enquiries@harriman-house.com
Website: www.harriman-house.com

ISBN: 9780857192776

British Library Cataloguing in Publication Data
A CIP catalogue record for this book can be obtained from the British Library.

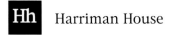

Printed and Bound in Great Britain by Marston Book Services Ltd, Didcot, Oxon

To Julie and Connor for making every day perfect.
I never thought life could be so amazing.

To my mother Annamarie for her continuing love, belief and inspiration.

To my father Friedrich. You always knew just what to say. I miss you every day.

ABOUT THE AUTHOR

Dr Adrian Manz earns his living as a professional analyst and stock trader. A successful professional equities trader for nearly a decade, he is the author of two books on the subject and the publisher of the *Intraday Trading Plan*, a nightly blueprint for the actions he plans to take in the markets on the following day.

Dr Manz is president of Peterson/Manz Trading Inc., co-general partner of Trireme Capital Advisors LLC, and the cofounder of **TraderInsight.com**. He is dedicated to providing trader education to anyone who is looking to add a new view of the markets to their repertoire. A regular public speaker at trading events, he is frequently interviewed about his trading style on radio and online.

Dr Manz is a graduate of the prestigious Peter F. Drucker Graduate School of Management and the School of Behavioral and Organizational Sciences at Claremont Graduate School. He and his wife, Dr Julie Peterson-Manz, live and work in Pacific Palisades, California.

Dr Manz can be contacted at adrian@traderinsight.com.

CONTENTS

Preface   ix

CHAPTER 1. INTRODUCTION   **1**

Structure of the Book   3

CHAPTER 2. THE NATURE OF VOLATILE MARKETS   **7**

Good Volatility   7
Bad Volatility   11
The Impact of Volatility on Trader Psychology   14
Summary   16

CHAPTER 3. THE BASICS   **17**

Two Strategies that Consistently Generate Profits   17
The Pullback Expansion Set-Up   17
The Consolidation Expansion Set-Up   20
Entry Rules and Position Management   22
Examples of the Basic Set-Up   23
   Harley Davidson Inc.   23
   Community Health Systems Inc.   25
   Companhia Paranaense Energy   26
   Family Dollar Stores Inc.   27
   Lincoln National Corporation   28
   BB&T Corporation   29
   Autonation Inc   30
Summary   31

CHAPTER 4. FILTERING THE BASIC SET-UP — 32

The Role of Volume and Per Cent Close in Defining the Set-Up — 32
    Amerigroup Corporation — 33
    Harley Davidson Inc. — 35
Summary — 40

CHAPTER 5. SETTING STOPS AND PROFIT TARGETS — 41

    KBR Inc — 44
    Iamgold Corp — 50
    Harman International Industries — 54
Summary — 59

CHAPTER 6. DAY TRADING NEWS EVENTS — 60

Trading News — 61
    Onyx Pharmaceuticals Inc — 64
    Nu Skin Enterprises Inc — 66
    Monster Beverage Corp. — 67
    Walter Energy Inc — 68
    Mosaic Corporation — 70
    SanDisk Corporation — 71
    Fusion-IO Inc — 72
Playing Both Sides of the News — 73
    Wellcare Health Plans Inc — 73
Summary — 74

CHAPTER 7. THE SINKER 52-WEEK-HIGH REVERSAL — 75

The Role of the Broader Markets — 78
    Netsuite Inc — 80
    Eli Lilly & Co. — 84
    Centene Corp — 86
    Plains All American Pipeline LP — 88
    Target Corp — 90
Summary — 92

CHAPTER 8. ESTABLISHING BIG-PICTURE POSITIONS   **93**

Amerigroup Corp   95
BMC Software Inc.   98
Harsco Corporation   101
Sherwin Williams Co   103
Summary   105

CHAPTER 9. THE VERTICALLY INTEGRATED TRADER   **106**

APPENDIX A. TRICKS OF THE TRADE   **109**

Parts of a Solid Plan   109
Amerigroup Corp   112
Healthnet   114
Ball Corporation   116
CBRE Group Inc   118
National Fuel Gas Co   120
Avnet Inc   122
Big Lots   124
Leucadia National Corp   126
NRG Energy Inc   128
Harley Davidson Inc   130
Universal Health Services Inc   132
Meritage Homes   134

APPENDIX B. TOOLS OF THE TRADE   **136**

PREFACE

WHEN A FRIEND suggested it was time for me to write another book, I replied that the book I thought needed to be written was too focused to pique the interest of most traders. What people were looking for were books that taught a *little* bit of a *lot* of trading strategies. But that wasn't the kind of book that would help them, so it wasn't the kind of book I wanted to write. Single chapters or sections do not provide enough space to develop the sorts of concepts that effective trading strategies rely on. Traders wind up buying many books with bits and pieces of the puzzle, and the big picture is left to their imagination.

All of that is great if you are in the business of selling books about trading. But I wanted the satisfaction of teaching people a *complete* trading method from start to finish. The more I talked to my friend, the more I became convinced that the book I thought needed to be written could be written – and there might just be enough readers getting frustrated with the scattergun approach to make it worthwhile. This book would focus the reader on a single, profitable trading paradigm. It would allow me to teach a winning system in depth. It would comprehensively answer trading questions that I had been asked again and again. You hold this book in your hands.

The expansion-of-range-and-volume set-up taught in this book is one of the best trading strategies that I use. Many of the traders that I have shared it with over the past 13 years tell me that they get excited every time they see it on a chart. They know that the pattern spells opportunity. When applied correctly, it can be the cornerstone of a profitable trading business. My goal in this book is to show readers how and why it works, and to demonstrate its utility for day, swing, and position traders.

What I present here is a trade secret. I will show readers that good trading strategies are not difficult to comprehend. I will demonstrate how a single construct can be the cornerstone of a profitable trading business. By the time readers have finished *Trade Secrets: Powerful Strategies for Volatile Markets,* they will agree that good strategies work in one time frame and rack up gains more often than losses. *Great* strategies, by contrast, are portable and can be applied in multiple time compressions to provide consistent returns.

The trade secret presented here shows clearly that the markets have entered a new era of trading. Traders need to discard conventional wisdom and pursue new avenues of thought. Traders need to stop wrapping their identities in terms like *day trader, swing trader, position trader* and *scalper.* They need to focus instead on being *professional traders.* A trader's job is to find and capitalise on opportunity in the markets in any time frame. Once the focus is shifted from time-centric trading to finding high-probability trades in the market, achieving profitability is just a matter of allowing opportunity to present itself.

As a buyer of the printed book of *Trade Secrets,* you can download the full eBook free of charge. Simply point your smartphone or tablet camera at this QR code or go to:

ebooks.harriman-house.com/tradesecrets

CHAPTER 1. Introduction

THE 1990S WERE a very good time to trade stocks, and I was lucky enough to start my business during the boom. I was luckier than I knew. I had decided to focus on the New York Stock Exchange. At the time, NYSE-listed securities were traded exclusively in the 'specialist' system, which allocated one security to a single specialist on the floor of the exchange. The firm this person represented was the only one transacting business in the stock, and it was very likely that the same person was on the other side of the trade every time I bought or sold a share. The notion of a human on the other side of every trade spelled opportunity to me.

As a psychologist, I thought that anticipating the actions of one NYSE specialist would be easier than trying to figure out what thirty NASDAQ market makers were doing. In order to succeed as a trader, I knew that I had to be on the same side of the trade as the insiders. It was their game. They had been playing it successfully for hundreds of years, and no matter what the bandits of the SOES (Small Order Execution System) and their brethren had to say, it was unlikely that the retail trader was ever going to beat the house in the long run. I essentially needed to predict which bets the house was willing to take and then take the same bet with my own money. That just seemed easier on the NYSE.

The theory proved correct: it was relatively easy to profit as the market soared higher. The NYSE was less volatile than the NASDAQ and allowed me to focus more on strategy and less on momentum. The impact of volatility on the lighter NYSE volume was also more predictable and could be discerned through chart and tape-reading techniques. These techniques provided predictive reliability rather than the hindsight of oscillators commonly employed on fast-moving NASDAQ stocks.

I had found a venue. That one 'lucky' decision meant that, as the market caved in under the weight of the dot-com bubble, I thrived. Meanwhile many of my counterparts in the markets folded up the tent and moved on to something else. I had learned to rely on price and volume data alone to predict future price and volume moves. This style, unfashionable at the time, led directly to my ability to prosper as a trader for 13 years.

Times have changed, and the NASDAQ and NYSE are now more similar than they ever were in the past. I think that the behaviour of stocks on the Big Board is still a bit easier to anticipate. But with the demise of countless momentum traders came the consolidation of the Electronic Communication Networks (ECNs) and a more level playing field on the NASDAQ. At the NYSE, much of the small order routing moved away from the specialist and was taken over by Archipelago (ARCA). The role of the specialist in the mundane was restricted. Nevertheless, the influence remains undeniable; large blocks of shares are still what make the market tick.

The blurring of the lines was inevitable. The 1990s allowed traders to profit by exploiting market inefficiencies. But efficient markets are the cornerstone of capitalism and the profit opportunity was longer lived than anyone could have expected. As the arena adjusted, the US equity exchanges began to look increasingly similar. The ability to profit by rapidly understanding the movement of price in efficient markets became the core competence required to play the game.

In fact, all of the world's exchanges have started to look very much alike. My techniques are successfully employed by traders all over the world, in stocks, options, futures, and currencies. All of them have learned to rely on *price as the ultimate arbiter of price*. And all of them see the market for what it really is – a place where attention to the footprints of money as it moves from one place to another can lead to the ability to profit substantially from opening gavel to closing bell.

I attribute my longevity and success as a trader to a way of seeing the markets. This perspective defines opportunity in such a way that makes it easy to spot statistically reliable set-ups on the fly. I have mathematically modeled my ideas many times. I have subjected them to sophisticated multivariate statistics and quantitative models. I have tried to make them purely systematic. Ultimately, I have concluded that the human brain is still better than any machine at anticipating the behaviour of people.

In this book, I focus on a set of volatility patterns that I know are efficient in finding and profiting from opportunities in today's markets. These have brought me tremendous success over the years. My core strategy was first discussed in my book *Beat the Street: A Trader's Guide to Consistently Profiting in the Markets*. In this book, I expand on the expansion-of-range-and-volume set-up and examine the many ways that I implement it in my trading.

The expansion-of-range-and-volume set-up is a powerful chart pattern that has proven enormously profitable during my years as a trader. It draws its ability to generate gains from the volatility that fuels the market itself. When volatility expands, set-ups illustrated in this book present opportunities to anticipate explosive moves. Getting on the correct side of the money flow is half the battle in trading. When developing a strategy, traders should always have this core idea at the forefront of their thinking. Traders want to be where the opportunities are. When the markets are moving, volatility- and expansion-based set-ups are definitely where the opportunities will be found.

Just before the new millennium, these set-ups were so common that all traders had to do was get up in the morning, enter the continuation move a few pennies beyond the previous day's extreme, wait a few minutes, and count the money. That falls under the category of 'all good things must come to an end', but volatility will always be part of trading. The key to capturing profits in today's market is to identify which moves are real, and which will result in pattern failure. The set-up identified in this book finds the breakouts that have all the ingredients to fuel a substantial continuation move, while eliminating most of the trades that would unnecessarily churn an account.

Structure of the Book

I have divided this book into eight distinct sections. In Chapter 2, I discuss the role of volatility in a trader's business. Not all volatility is the same. One type leads to profits, while its counterpart leads to losses, which can sometimes be catastrophic. By learning to employ a few simple filtering criteria, traders can learn to take advantage of potentially profitable volatility, and head for the hills (or the beach in my case) when the threatening iteration appears in the markets.

In Chapter 3, I revisit the basic expansion set-up as I defined it in 2003. Presenting the rules for that strategy ensures that the groundwork for the rest of the strategies in this book are firmly in place.

In Chapter 4, I redefine and provide additional filtering criteria for the basic expansion set-up. While the original ideas still work very well, I have found that market behaviour has changed just enough over the years that some additional criteria help to maintain, or even increase, the profitability that is possible with the pattern. My priority is to keep trading simple: there are no complicated mathematical formulas, oscillators or other indicators added to the set-up. Instead, I focus on the role of price action and volume in making a great strategy even better.

In Chapter 5, I look at how to set profit targets and stop losses using natural support and resistance at a confluence of key technical zones, such as Fibonacci levels and floor trader pivots. I also describe how to trail stops to protect profits once a position is moving in my favour.

Chapter 6 takes time compression to the extreme. It demonstrates how the pattern can be successfully employed to spot intraday trading candidates after takeover chatter begins to circulate on the news wires. News wires have become increasingly popular with intraday traders. Although the information provided by these services is the most timely and relevant available, I have found in my discussions with hundreds of traders that most cannot figure out how to use the information to generate profits. The expansion strategy presented here will illustrate how I apply the concepts to the micro intraday trading environment to capitalise on discrete, easily identifiable, and regularly occurring news events. Traders who are comfortable operating in the tighter time compression of an intraday chart will find that the ideas presented here will add a strategy with significant potential to their trading repertoire.

Chapter 7 presents a variation of the pattern that I have never before published. When markets reach tops, this set-up has proven extremely reliable, generating profits with unprecedented accuracy. I call it the *sinker set-up*. When it appears on a daily chart, I have extreme confidence. In recent years, it correctly predicted major market reversals in stocks 90% of the times that the pattern triggered, generating consistent profits for me and subscribers to my *Around The Horn Trading Plan*. The sinker set-up is another example of how important it is that the patterns relied on by traders are robust enough to handle varying market environments and maintain their ability to profit. While stocks may or may not be at a market top when this book is being read, I can predict with 100% confidence that stocks will be at a market top again sometime in the foreseeable future. When that happens, the sinker variation of the expansion-of-range-and-volume strategy will be a tool traders will be happy to have in their arsenal.

In Chapter 8, I present a variation on the strategy that allows traders to capitalise on easily identifiable swing and position-trading opportunities. This adds an entirely new dimension to the trading strategy. While the original intraday version is designed primarily to generate income, the swing and position trading set-up is suitable for individuals who are looking to build wealth. Whether implemented by the individual trader for a private account, or by an institutional trader looking to build wealth for clients, this strategy is capable of generating substantial returns when employed in big-picture trading.

Chapter 9 focuses on how the face of trading has changed. The markets have entered a new era in which it is not sufficient for traders to focus on one style of trading, one time compression, or a single view of the markets. The economy has changed. The world has changed. And the markets have changed with them. The trader who is not able to see the forest for the trees needs to prepare to be lost in the woods. Those who still believe that a focus on a single market or time frame is the only way to make a living should seek other employment opportunities. Today's markets require an understanding and intuitiveness that was never a prerequisite in the past. If a trader cannot find opportunity in what I discuss as the *vertical markets*, then the likelihood of success diminishes significantly.

Appendix A contains my actual trading journal of all the expansion set-ups that occurred in January 2012. This was a high-volatility month, and many good set-ups occurred and triggered. I show all of the set-ups along with all of my journal entries regarding entries, taking profits, trailing stops, and ultimately how, why and when each trade was closed.

In Appendix B, I discuss setting up a trading work area. I discuss what I consider to be the essential components to have on screen for the full range of equipment traders may be using. I show my own computer workstation, which implements some major horsepower. I work through all of the possibilities, from what I think is needed to trade on a laptop to how I manage data on eight monitors. By doing so, I hope to answer the questions about equipment and software that I hear all the time but rarely see anyone address. After reading this section, traders should have some very good ideas as to what configuration of equipment will help run a trading business.

There are many profitable trading ideas to consider and internalise while reading this book. The focus on multiple time frames, trading style, and volatility represent a paradigm shift for many readers. It has also represented a shift for me, but I believe that failure to change with the market will result in failure in the market.

CHAPTER 2.
The Nature of Volatile Markets

VOLATILITY IS THE quintessential double-edged sword. With it, markets can be difficult to navigate and frightening to trade. Without it, there would be no markets. Volatility is the man behind the curtain. It creates opportunity. It defines where traders will find profit. And it defines where they will experience loss. Volatility is found in two forms. For our purposes, these forms can be easily identified by any student of the market as:

1. good volatility

2. bad volatility.

While my characterisation may seem to trivialise the importance of volatility, I assure you that I have the utmost respect for it. In this chapter, I explain that there is a distinct difference between the good and the bad forms. Good volatility can lead to profits and the bad to losses, but more importantly, traders who take the time to acknowledge this distinction can significantly hedge their risks.

I will define the parameters for each type of volatility in the following sections. I will also provide some examples of each at work in the market to clarify the nature of the dichotomy.

Good Volatility

Understanding the concept of volatility does not require an advanced degree in statistics. I am also not referring to the volatility construct measured in options models. Rather, what I am referring to is a market that is trending and the forces that cause the trend to persist. The extent to which a trader needs to understand the mathematics of the construct is limited to the basics of mean reversion. Good volatility will expand and contract around an average value.

When something is mean-reverting, it naturally gravitates back to its average value and constantly orbits that value in quantifiable and predictable ways. In Figure 2.1, I illustrate this with the horizontal line being the average volatility value for a given time frame, and the dark circles being the periods of high volatility. The lighter circles represent times when volatility is reverting to the average value. Notice that the movement around the average is smooth and predictable. This is a key characteristic of good volatility, and represents a period of opportunity in the markets.

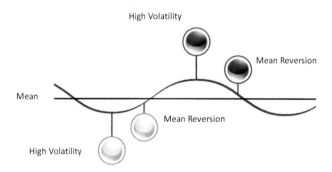

FIGURE 2.1

Good volatility is caused by the psychology of fear and greed. It is generally more evident when a market is collapsing than when it is gaining value. When markets are on the rise, greed acts as a powerful motivator, and is capable of fuelling substantial volatility. Investors see markets moving higher; most will ultimately pile in, creating a self-fulfilling, explosive price move that will ultimately reverse and create massive losses. Though greed will definitely propel markets, fear is where the action is, as most investors are much more concerned with the prospect of abject poverty than they are with the lure of countless riches.

When a downtrend is firmly in place, savvy short sellers can smell the blood in the water as the previously greedy investors transform into fearful liquidators. The good volatility in a market collapse always provides more opportunity than its counterpart in the rising market. Falling prices can typically deconstruct in a month what it took rising prices a year to build. Although most retail investors have been trained by the pros to avoid it, the short side of the market is definitely a place full of good volatility and great opportunity. In order to earn a living in the market, traders need to work with the market and avoid fighting the tape. Buy when the market is trending higher. Short when the market is trending lower. And avoid the market when good volatility in a definite trend cannot be found.

Trends give an observable purpose to price action. When shares of a company's stock are trending higher or lower, the best predictor of what price will do tomorrow is what it did today. A valid trend should be obvious to the naked eye. My general rule is that if finding something requires an indicator, then it is probably better not found.

A trend should unfold on a chart in a manner that makes it easy to spot. Note in Figure 2.2 that the trend in the Dow Jones Industrials during most of 2011 and 2012 was never in doubt. The index had two quarters of solid growth, a quarter of consolidation, and then another quarter in which the trend was solidly higher. The conclusion from the chart is that the third quarter of 2011 through the third quarter of 2012 was an uptrending period.

FIGURE 2.2 – DOW JONES INDUSTRIAL AVERAGE (I)
RealTick® graphics used with permission of RealTick LLC. ©1986-2012 RealTick LLC. All Rights reserved.
RealTick® is registered trademark of RealTick LLC.

If a major trend is at work, it should be observable in multiple time frames. Pullbacks and consolidations should be evident in the shorter time compressions before they manifest in the bigger picture. As the trend persists in the longer compressions (weekly bars on a chart for example), the pullbacks and consolidations in the shorter compressions (daily bars) should be followed by periods of high volatility in the form of wide-range bars that expand price action in the direction of the bigger picture chart. This is evident in Figure 2.2, which shows the trend in the Dow Jones Industrials taking short pauses and then expanding in volatile moves in its journey from 10,400 to 13,400.

Good volatility manifests as exaggerated and predictable price behaviour. It can easily be confirmed across time frames. There should be periods of decreased activity during consolidation or retracement phases, followed by an increase in the travel range of the bars on a chart after these phases mature. The weekly chart of the 2011–12 Dow Jones Industrials in Figure 2.3 shows how obvious a trend can be.

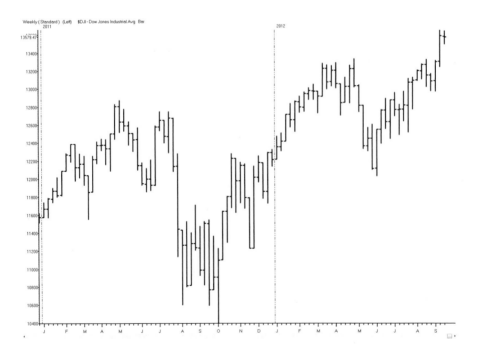

FIGURE 2.3 – DOW JONES INDUSTRIAL AVERAGE (II)
RealTick by Townsend Analytics, Ltd.

Bad Volatility

While good volatility helps traders predict significant extensions of gains and losses made during trending market moves, bad volatility adds nothing to the picture but noise. That noise usually comes in the form of whipsaw moves higher and lower, and sideways congestion moves that appear to indicate that the market cannot pick a direction. In either case, losses can pile up as traders and investors are stopped in and out of positions. The price action offers no predictive validity in determining what may come next.

A useful way to conceptualise the distinction between price behaviour in good volatility and price behaviour in bad volatility is to remember that good volatility occurs in the presence of a discernible trend, and results in wider-range price bars as the volatility increases. Bad volatility results in similar increases in the travel range of individual price bars, but the moves occur without a trend pushing price higher or lower. Whatever time frame a trader is working in, there will be little evidence of strong directionality when bad volatility is at work. The lack of directional movement is what I referred to as noise a moment ago, and experienced traders can spot the condition on a chart with little effort.

Those who wish to use computerised scanning to identify and eliminate noisy markets or stocks from their screening process can use Wilder's ADX (Average Directional Indicator)[1] when making their first cut. Readings below 20 accompanied by larger-than-average range are indicative of non-trending conditions. Readings above 20 indicate that conditions are changing. When that reading occurs along with wide range price bars, a tradeable trend may be underway.

Raising the threshold to an ADX of 30 increases the amount of trending price action that the indicator requires. This will also narrow the list of trading candidates for traders who are comfortable letting a machine do a little bit of their homework for them. I like to use this technique with my scanning software MetaStock to narrow the number of stocks in my basket to a manageable group. The popular MetaStock add-on module for my strategies allows me to automate the process even further by filtering the bad volatility candidates out of the universe of stocks I will consider.

---

[1] Wilder, J. Wells (1978). *New Concepts in Technical Trading Systems*. Trend Research.

Many traders have tried to use variations of ADX in the presence of bad volatility as a way to predict trend reversals. While I have, on occasion, seen congestion ranges and random volatility resolve with a big picture reversal, my experience in the markets over the past dozen years tells me that this type of volatility rarely offers any assistance in anticipating directionality. I have known many traders who have tried to convince me that they could use market noise to predict the future. I have, however, never met one who could do it without that future already being plotted on the chart. It is only with the benefit of hindsight that a compelling argument for a systematic approach to random volatility can be made. And since hindsight is generally accepted to be 20/20, the addition of the volatility- or congestion-based systems offers little utility in my view.

Bad volatility is clearly at work on the daily chart in Figure 2.4. Price action is badly defined and is randomly moving the Dow Jones Industrials.

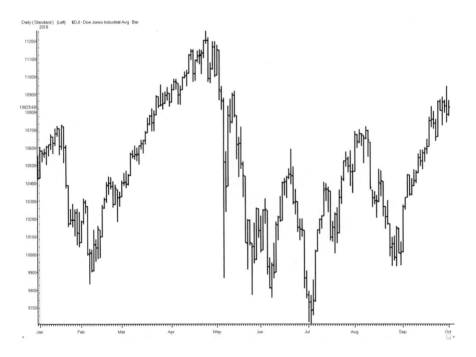

FIGURE 2.4 – DOW JONES INDUSTRIAL AVERAGE (III)
RealTick by Townsend Analytics, Ltd.

The price action on the daily chart in Figure 2.4, however, is not leading the weekly data (Figure 2.5), which is characteristic of bad volatility. Both time frames are choppy, and neither provides good insight into what is coming next. Speculators may or may not be correct in making their directional bets for the balance of 2010, but the important point to consider is that the activity during the volatility phase did nothing to assist traders in predicting the subsequent move.

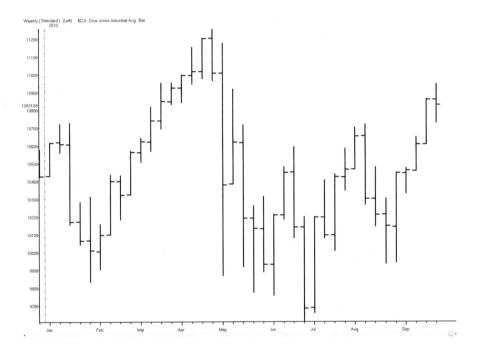

FIGURE 2.5 – DOW JONES INDUSTRIAL AVERAGE (IV)
RealTick by Townsend Analytics, Ltd.

All this is not to imply that volatility in its bad form is not valuable. Quite on the contrary, it tells me when to stay out of the market and take a break from trading. No matter how many trading set-ups I find during one of these periods, I ignore them. I know in advance that the ability of a stock to follow through is more a matter of chance than good strategy when its price behaviour is determined by bad volatility. This precludes using such set-ups as part of an informed trading plan.

The Impact of Volatility on Trader Psychology

I can say with complete certainty that trader psychology accounts for at least half of the successes or failures that an individual will experience in dealing with the markets. I can also say with complete confidence that one of the principle causes of psychological impasse in trading is a misunderstanding of the construct of volatility. Far too many traders feel that it is necessary to be in the market every day. I have a separate email folder devoted to storing the acid-tongued emails that I receive from new subscribers when there are days or weeks in which few set-ups or triggers occur. Americans have been conditioned to accept a work ethic that mandates showing up every day even if there is nothing to do. The consequences of that being carried over into the world of financial trading can be disastrous.

Most of the emails insinuate that the absence of a plan indicates a failure to plan. Nothing could be further from the truth. Any day that I have no set-ups on my trading plan is a day that there were either no solid patterns, or a day where the bad volatility was dominating the environment and making it impossible to plan entries that would prove reliable.

Pattern trading methodologies almost never benefit from the bad type of volatility. Yet many new traders refuse to consider its role in hampering their ability to succeed. This leads to psychological discomfort, which leads in turn to second-guessing a methodology. That is where the real trouble begins.

When traders misattribute the cause of a loss, they run the risk of a permanent attribution error that will cause them to second-guess entries and stops, avoid entering trades, cut profits short, and let losses run. Volatility is a key piece of the puzzle. And when it is missing from the evaluation process, uncertainty and doubt frequently cause traders to make some bad decisions.

A trader may construct a plan without considering the impact of volatility on price behaviour and that the underlying volatility happens to be the bad variety. The next day, an expansion set-up gets the trader into a long position, and choppy price behaviour causes a full stop-out. Now, if this happens on several occasions, and if the trader is never aware that volatility had a role in the loss that was experienced, a series of events is likely to unfold:

1. The next time the same pattern-type triggers an entry, the trader will hesitate to enter the position. There will be a cognitive push to try to find signs of the same activity that caused the previous losses.

2. The trader will sometimes guess right and sometimes guess wrong, but will generally get into a habit of missing entries and then looking for confirmation that the decision to avoid the trade was justified by the avoidance of a loss. This is facilitated by a powerful and debilitating psychological phenomenon known as intermittent reinforcement. Once this construct shapes behaviour, it can be difficult to extinguish. This explains much of why traders keep making the same mistakes over and over in an effort to protect their capital.

3. Eventually, trades that are perceived as safe will be entered with mixed results, and trades that are perceived as dangerous will be avoided. The trades that look dangerous will be seen as such because they appear volatile. The gains that would have been generated with good volatility are ignored or construed as unpredictable. There will be no assessment of whether the volatility is of the good or bad variety, and the reinforcement of avoiding losses is usually so strong that it completely overrides the desire to make a profit.

All of this happens because the original losing trades were volatile prior to creating a loss. There was no identification of the bad volatility at the time, so now all volatility is construed as bad. If there is any doubt as to whether this is plausible, a little soul-searching is in order. I cannot overstate the number of times in the past decade a subscriber to my trading plan has told me that a trade was missed. When I say, "I got it. Most everyone else seemed to get it." The response is either "I hesitated," or "It just didn't look like it was going to go."

The same psychological twist causes traders to relocate established stops and profit targets, which books winning trades early and lets losing trades run. Basically, it is psychologically reinforcing to take a win and psychologically damaging to take a loss. The reinforcement is frequently sought as soon as possible, while the loss is avoided so long that many traders' portfolios are composed entirely of their worst trades. "It will come back eventually." "I'll exit at break-even." "I still like the stock."

"It has such a high dividend yield." The preceding quotes are the four worst reasons to own a stock. Ultimately, the mistake can be avoided entirely by simply acknowledging and respecting market volatility.

Summary

The value of volatility in the planning of every trade and the trading of every plan is indisputable. In the absence of volatile markets, trading for a living would not be possible. Volatility is the engine of market behaviour. But even on the smoothest ride, there is a squeaky wheel. The influence of both good and bad volatility need to be acknowledged if one is to be a successful trader. Were it not for volatility, we would all just be better off investing our accounts in an index and waiting for a slow steady move to create a long-term gain.

In the presence of good volatility, trading the markets for income and wealth accumulation becomes a viable occupation. Moves in the direction of, and counter to, an underlying trend can generate significant profits during periods in which a buy-and-hold strategy would do nothing to build an account.

The main point I am making here is that traders need to acknowledge the impact volatility has on the positions they are considering in order to be successful in the markets. Traders should initiate trades only when the underlying volatility appears to offer assistance in achieving profit objectives, and avoid trades when volatility threatens to whipsaw positions.

CHAPTER 3. The Basics

THE FOLLOWING IS a review of the core set-ups as defined in my book *Beat the Street: A Trader's Guide to Consistently Profiting in the Markets*. These patterns have been bread-and-butter trades in my account for 13 years and I believe that, when applied correctly, they can be a core component in any trading strategy.

Two Strategies that Consistently Generate Profits

Like much in the markets, expansion set-ups prove most reliable when preceded by an orderly event. When I am flipping charts in search of trading candidates, I look for these orderly events in the form of a pullback or a definite price consolidation. These provide evidence that an expansion move will likely lead to profits. The first step in understanding what I am looking for is to examine ideal examples of each and discuss the forces at work behind the scenes that can differentiate a high-probability trade from average set-ups. The differences between a potential winner and loser are often subtle, but once traders have looked at enough set-ups, the good ones will jump right off the screen as traders organise their trading plans.

The Pullback Expansion Set-Up

The first variation of the pattern works best when the trading day that completes the set-up comes on the heels of a pullback in a major trending move. Traders push price to an extreme and then back away as the stock, option or future becomes too expensive (in the case of a long candidate) or too cheap (in the case of a short candidate). A reversal that moves to one of the major Fibonacci ratios, a significant moving average, or a level of considerable prior support and resistance creates an environment in which many investors and traders look for a reason to get into the market. If they enter a trade at the same time as major institutional money, the expansion set-up on a pullback materialises and presents an opportunity to generate some quick profits from a fast intraday move.

The example in Figure 3.1 below illustrates the ideal set-up for the long entry. The rules are as follows:

1. The precursor for pattern formation is a pullback in an uptrend.

2. The stock breaks out of the pullback in the direction of the original trend. The move is the widest range of the past ten days, and volume on the breakout day is higher than the average daily volume during the pullback.

3. On the trigger day, enter .10 above the high of the breakout bar. Stops should be ratcheted up as soon as the trade is profitable. Close the position by the end of the trading day.

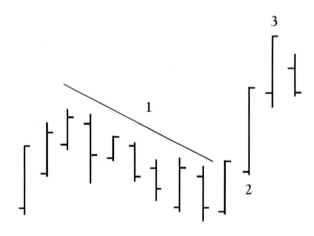

FIGURE 3.1 – LONG ENTRY SET-UP

Destructive price action tends to occur with much more conviction than its constructive counterpart. When price starts falling, the opportunity offered by the set-up can be increased significantly. To capitalize on this, traders need to engage in a short sale.

Shorting stocks is sometimes confusing, but the process is really very simple. Borrow shares of a stock from a broker and promise to return them at a later time. Sell the shares at the current price, and if the price falls, buy back the stock and return it to the broker. The amount that the stock fell is the profit. If price rises and the stock is bought back at a higher level, the amount of the stock's appreciation is the loss.

The rules for a short sale are illustrated in Figure 3.2 and are as follows:

1. The precursor for pattern formation is a pullback in a downtrend.

2. The stock breaks down from the pullback in the direction of the original trend. The move represents the widest range of the past ten days, and volume on the breakdown day should be higher than the average daily volume during the pullback.

3. On the trigger day, enter .10 below the low of the breakdown bar. Stops should be ratcheted down as soon as the trade is profitable. Close the position by the end of the trading day.

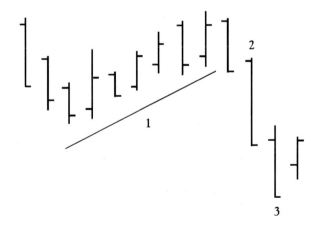

FIGURE 3.2 – SHORT SALE SET-UP

The Consolidation Expansion Set-Up

Stock prices consolidate for a reason. Sometimes a particular market has reached equilibrium. Other times traders are trying to figure out whether to pile on or head for the door. Either of these motives can ultimately lead to substantial trading profits if traders carefully watch for them. The second expansion-of-range-and-volume set-up happens when a consolidation ends and gives way to a sharp move.

The example in Figure 3.3 illustrates the long entry. The rules are as follows:

1. The precursor for pattern formation is a discernible trend. The stock must stop trending and form at least a five-day consolidation range.

2. A break to the upside occurs, taking price out of the channel either in the direction of the original trend or counter to it. The move must represent the widest range of the past ten days. Volume should be higher on the breakout day than the average daily volume during the consolidation period.

3. Enter .10 above the high of the breakout bar. Stops should be ratcheted up as soon as the trade is profitable. Close the position by the end of the trading day.

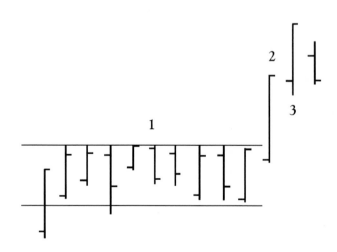

FIGURE 3.3 – LONG ENTRY SET-UP

In Figure 3.4, the rules of the long entry are inverted for the short set-up. The rules for the short set-up are as follows:

1. The precursor for pattern formation is a discernible trend. The stock must stop trending and form at least a five-day consolidation range.

2. A break to the downside occurs, taking price out of the channel either in the direction of the original trend or counter to it. The move must represent the widest range of the past ten days. Volume should be higher on the breakout day than the average daily volume during the consolidation period.

3. Enter .10 below the low of the breakout bar. Stops should be ratcheted down as soon as the trade is profitable. Close the position by the end of the trading day.

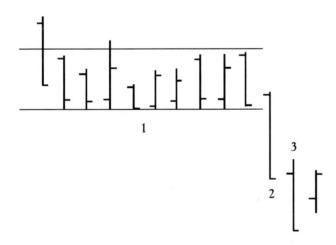

FIGURE 3.4 – SHORT SALE SET-UP

These are the fundamental building blocks of the set-up. Understanding how they operate is essential to learning and applying the refinements I explain later. Make sure that you understand both pattern set-ups and all four pattern applications (pullback long entry, pullback short entry, consolidation long entry and consolidation short entry) prior to reading any further.

Entry Rules and Position Management

"Plan the trade – trade the plan" was the motto in my trading when most of Wall Street was more inclined to shoot from the hip. I still plan everything, and that includes intraday trade management once a position triggers.

1. The first entry is automatic. If the entry price is hit, the trade is on.

2. If price moves .10 against the position prior to moving .10 in its favour, the trade is scratched for a .10 loss. This rule is suspended during high volatility.

3. Price must travel at least .08 through the entry price before turning around for a second entry (or first entry after an opening gap). Should the price touch the entry price, without going the required .08, but then go at least to the 50% line, the missed opportunity counts as an entry.

4. After two .10 scratch losses, the entry price moves to one cent beyond the day's high (for longs) or low (for shorts). This rule is not applicable after opening gaps, because the entry price is being moved to one cent beyond the day's high or low. The entry price is moved a maximum of five cents, meaning the trade moved a maximum of four cents in its favour before reversing.

5. If a trade moves 50% of the distance from the planned entry to the initial profit target, the stop is moved to break-even.

6. If a trade hits the stop loss, the trade is exited. A second entry will be taken if the entry price is hit again.

7. After second entry, an *Around the Horn* set-up becomes a discretionary *Stocks to Watch* set-up where a new protective stop based on the intraday price action must be found for another entry.

8. There are a maximum of three .10 scratch loss trades.

Examples of the Basic Set-Up

Real market examples are always better learning tools than textbook examples. So in the remainder of this text, I make extensive use of charts that represent actual trades. By the end, readers should have seen enough charts to firmly reinforce the concepts and start looking for the set-ups themselves.

I will build on the simple rules just explained to develop more refined and predictable pattern set-up criteria, but first I will look at examples based on what I have already covered to reinforce the core set-up. These are original examples from *Beat the Street* and from my *Around The Horn Trading Plan* (a trading service available at **www.traderinsight.com**). After reviewing these, I further develop the logic behind the successful range expansion entry.

I examine many actual expansion-of-range-and-volume trading set-ups throughout this book. Readers will almost certainly notice that some of the trades that I have chosen date back a few years. One of the first editors who looked at this manuscript commented on this and asked if I was unable to find more recent examples. I explained that the chapter contents are intended to provide the reader with evidence of how robust this trading set-up is and how well the pattern holds up over time. I have been trading it daily for nearly 13 years, and it is as prevalent today as it was when I started.

In order to satisfy those readers who would like to see more set-ups and see both winners and losers, I have included many more samples in Appendix A of this book. There readers will find all the expansion set-ups that triggered entries in January 2012 as they appeared in my *Around The Horn Trading Plan*. I also have provided the narratives from my own trading diary regarding the management of the trades once they triggered.

Harley Davidson Inc.

Harley Davidson Inc. (HOG) spent most of 2011 trading in a volatile and congested range. Trading in HOG started to settle down late in the year, and by early 2012 price movement in HOG was orderly and predictable. The first sign that HOG was ready to generate some solid trading results came when the stock began an accumulation and mark-up cycle in January (Figure 3.5).

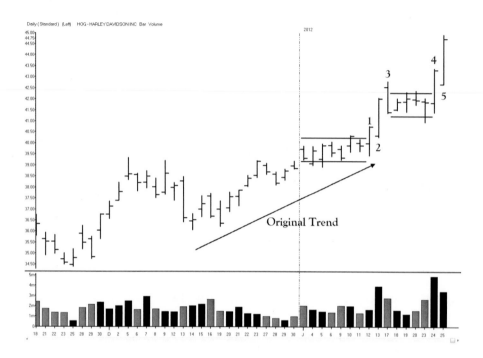

FIGURE 3.5 – HARLEY DAVIDSON INC.
RealTick by Townsend Analytics, Ltd.

1. A two-week trend consolidates in an accumulation range. HOG makes an expansion-of-range-and-volume move higher. The upper boundary of the range is clearly violated, and the stock makes a strong close.

2. HOG triggers and trades smoothly to the planned profit target.

3. After gapping higher, HOG closes lower. A five-day consolidation range forms as traders accumulate the stock.

4. Another expansion-of-range-and-volume move sets up, and a trade is planned for the following session.

5. An entry .10 above the high of the bar that created the set-up leads to $1.40 per share in profits on the session.

Community Health Systems Inc.

Shares of Community Health Systems Inc. (CYH) spent most of 2011 in a steep decline. CYH moved from a high of $42 early in the year to a low of $14.61 by mid October. A series of analyst upgrades late in the year set the stage for an accumulation and mark-up cycle in 2012. In Figure 3.6, CYH shows the tell-tale signs of an exhaustion move, as a gap is followed by two waves of price action that fail to make a new high.

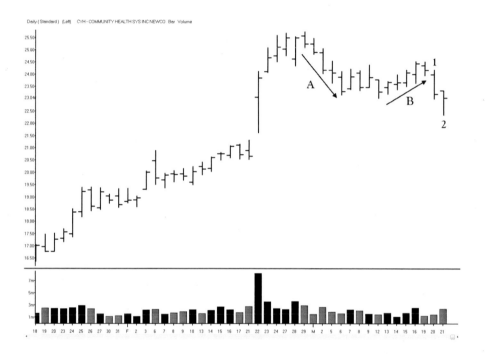

FIGURE 3.6 – COMMUNITY HEALTH SYSTEMS INC.
RealTick by Townsend Analytics, Ltd.

1. After posting a 2012 high in March, CYH moves lower (A) and attempts to pull higher (B). The pullback fails to make a new high, and CYH makes an expansion-of-range-and-volume move lower. A short-sale trade is planned with a $22.90 entry. The profit target on the trade is at $22.37 daily support.

2. An entry trigger is followed by a move to the profit target. By the end of the session, CYH retraces the move and closes flat. The volatile nature of the

expansion-of-range-and-volume pattern often leads to reversals such as this, and this volatility also frequently leads to gaps opposing the original move in the following sessions. It is precisely for this reason that I do not advocate overnight positions in trades that were planned for an intraday time frame.

Companhia Paranaense Energy

American depositary receipts can be difficult to trade, but shares of Companhia Paranaense Energy (ELP) are frequently on my trading plan, as the moves they make are nearly as smooth as most NYSE securities. When ELP made multiple swing moves with lower highs in March of 2012, I was eager to capitalise on any solid expansion-of-range-and-volume set-up on the short side of the market.

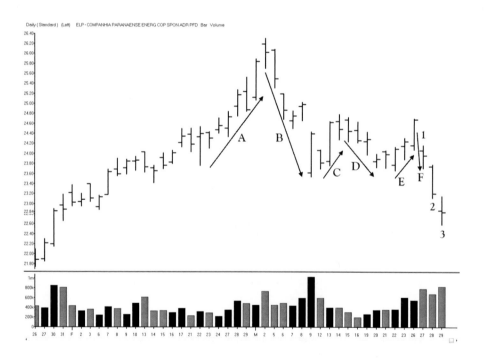

FIGURE 3.7 – COMPANHIA PARANAENSE ENERGY
RealTick by Townsend Analytics, Ltd.

1. ELP made a series of swing moves (A–B, C–D, E–F) that retested an earlier breakout level. While February support initially seemed substantial enough to

hold the stock above 23.50, increasing volume on the E–F sell-off indicated a potential move lower in the making.

2. An expansion-of-range-and-volume move takes ELP below support and sets up a $23.02 entry for the following session.

3. ELP opens and quickly trades to the $22.71 initial profit target.

Family Dollar Stores Inc.

When all else fails, people like to invest their money in businesses that they can understand. Family Dollar Stores Inc. (FDO) is one such company. In March of 2012, the news media was buzzing with stories about recession-weary consumers looking for bargains. Profit opportunities for deep discounters in America seemed to be expanding, and this had many financial pundits pointing to retailers like Family Dollar Stores as a good place to invest. This got FDO shares moving. And when FDO starts a directional expansion, the activity tends to draw traders in from the sidelines rather quickly.

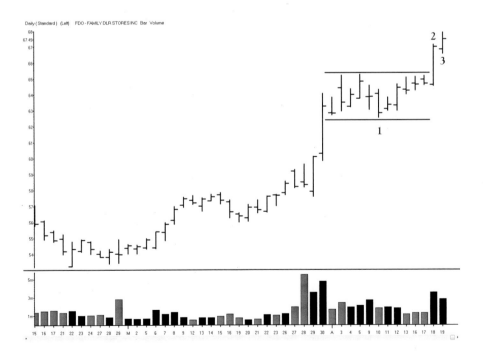

FIGURE 3.8 – FAMILY DOLLAR STORES INC.
RealTick by Townsend Analytics, Ltd.

1. Positive media coverage, analyst upgrades and positive statements by company executives moved FDO sharply higher in an expansion-of-range-and-volume move that was followed by a two-week consolidation.

2. Another expansion-of-range-and-volume set-up forms as FDO moves higher, clearing resistance at the top of the consolidation range.

3. The stock triggers a $67.25 entry, .10 above the previous session's high. The position is closed at the $67.90 initial profit target.

Lincoln National Corporation

Shares of Lincoln National Corporation (LNC) spent much of the second quarter of 2012 unwinding the gains that they had posted in the first quarter of the year. Earlier price appreciation had occurred against a backdrop of takeover chatter and upgrades that propelled the stock higher on heavy daily volume. When news about LNC dried up in April, so did interest in its stock. Price started falling as the reality of the company's financial situation became clear to investors who had earlier pinned their hopes for big gains on the possibility of a buyout.

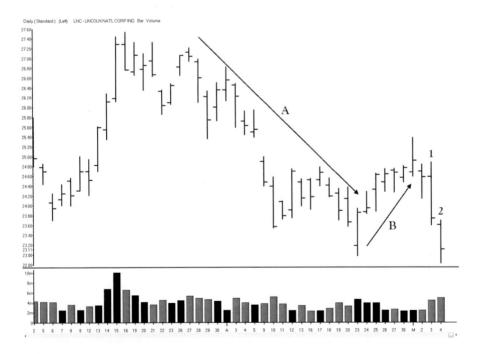

FIGURE 3.9 – LINCOLN NATIONAL CORPORATION
RealTick by Townsend Analytics, Ltd.

1. A persistent sell-off (A) moves shares of LNC lower by 10%. The stock attempts to climb higher over the course of a week's trading (B). Overhead supply pushes price lower in an expansion-of-range-and-volume move. The short-sale entry is planned for a tick at $23.50 the following session. The daily support target on the trade is $23.04, and the intraday resistance stop loss is at $23.85.

2. On the trigger day, LNC travels through the entry price and proceeds to make a waterfall move that takes the stock to $22.80 for a profit extension and an exit after a lengthy intraday consolidation range is violated at $22.90.

BB&T Corporation

Real estate services firm BB&T Corporation (BBT) tends to make trending moves that last several months before reversing course. The predictable nature of the stock's directional moves make BBT a good candidate for intraday trading, and when a sell-off left the stock in a distribution range, a solid opportunity for profit was at hand.

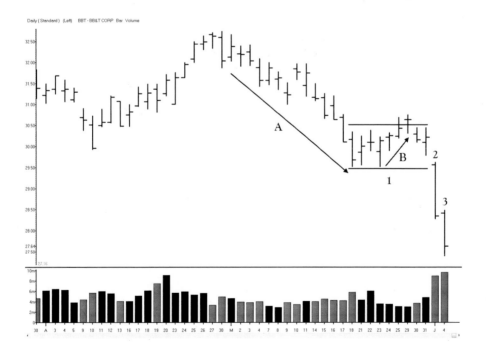

FIGURE 3.10 – BB&T CORPORATION
RealTick by Townsend Analytics, Ltd.

1. A three-week trending move (A) takes BBT lower and leaves it in a distribution range. The stock consolidates and attempts to climb up and out of the range it has formed over the course of a week's trading (B). Overhead supply pushes price back into the range on heavy volume.

2. An expansion-of-range-and-volume day has us ready to short the stock the following day on a violation of the $28.28 low.

3. We short the stock at $28.18. Over the course of the session, BBT trades as low as $27.40.

Autonation Inc

Automotive retail stocks have always made frequent appearances on my trading plan, as stocks in the sector can compound intraday gains very quickly. Many traders watch this sector, and this generally adds fuel to any momentum that exerts itself during the session. When Autonation announced a 45% increase in year-over-year auto sales in May 2012, the stage was set for some very good intraday moves.

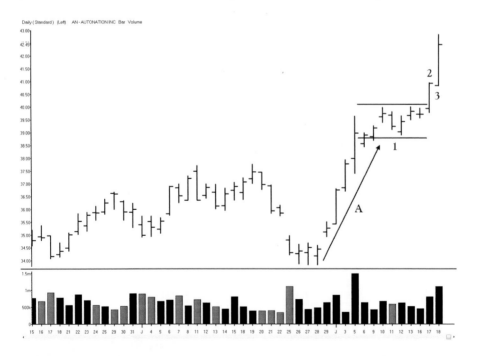

FIGURE 3.11 – AUTONATION
RealTick by Townsend Analytics, Ltd.

1. Autonation (AN) shares posted a 15% gain after the release of the company's sales figures for the year (A). The stock consolidated for just over a week, frequently testing the top of the accumulation range.

2. The stock makes a move out of the consolidation on heavy volume and I plan a $41.06 long entry. Although the set-up bar does not have the widest range of the past ten sessions, I included it on my trading plan. This is because the spirit of the set-up is definitely represented in the recent price action. I have included this example because I think it is very important to emphasise the importance of flexible thinking when it comes to generating profits in trading. Set-ups do not need to be picture-perfect to offer good opportunities.

3. On the trigger day, AN moves more than $1.50 per share in our favour.

Summary

The set-up that I called expansion-of-range-and-volume in *Beat the Street* is every bit as valid and lucrative today as it was when I first wrote about it in 2003. Everything I wrote then is true today. The fact that the book is in its sixth printing and fourth edition says much about the reception it has received from traders around the world.

My simple approach to trading remains unchanged. But I have learned that there are additional filters that can narrow the number of candidates and improve the results of many of my set-ups. In the following chapters I explore the filters that apply to the expansion-of-range-and-volume set-up.

CHAPTER 4.
Filtering the Basic Set-Up

The Role of Volume and Per Cent Close in Defining the Set-Up

I AM A BIG advocate of 'simpler is better'. The basic pattern rules will generate many good trading candidates every day. But if we add some simple volume criteria to our selection process, the odds of success are significantly improved. There are two volume filters and a closing range criterion that are useful in filtering the set-ups.

I use the following rules for both the pullback and consolidation set-up and have found that they are very effective in narrowing my nightly list of set-ups to a manageable number of high-probability trades.

1. The volume on the expansion day should be significant when compared to the volume of the lookback period. In the case of the pullback set-up, this means that the volume on the breakout day should be higher than the average volume during the pullback. For the consolidation set-up, volume on the breakout day should be higher than the average volume during the consolidation.

2. The volume going into the market close should be significant when compared to the rest of the trading session. I look at a five-minute chart and assess what happened as we approached the closing bell. If there was heavy volume and a steady move to the extreme of the price bar, there is a good chance that institutions, investors and traders failed to fill their orders. They were looking for an opportunity to buy or sell all the shares they could, and a heavy volume close will indicate that the pressure on the stock will continue the next morning.

3. The stock should finish the day's trading in the extreme 25% of the price bar and in the direction of the potential entry. So for a long set-up, I want to see

the closing price in the top quarter of the bar. A short should close in the bottom quarter. The closer to the absolute high or low the stock closes, the better.

Amerigroup Corporation

Some examples will help clarify the benefit of adding the additional filters to the screening process. Look at the daily chart of Amerigroup Corporation (AGP) in Figure 4.1. We see that the set-up came on the heels of a consolidation after a two-week trend and occurred on a high-volume day.

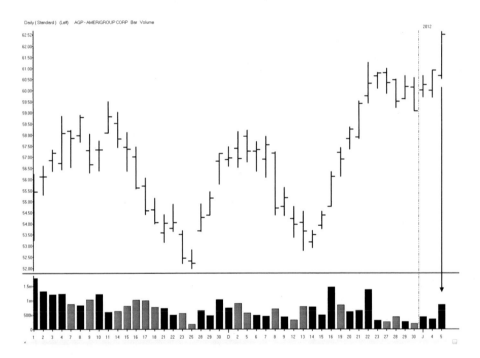

FIGURE 4.1 – AMERIGROUP CORPORATION (I)
RealTick by Townsend Analytics, Ltd.

It is always important to consider why a stock is pulling back or consolidating when evaluating a potential set-up. In this case, AGP gapped significantly lower in August of 2011 and struggled to regain ground for the rest of the year (Figure 4.2). The stock was trending higher and consolidating gains from October through December. AGP then hit a level of resistance that represented an area at which many traders had previously purchased and supported shares in the company. When the level was breached, an expansion-of-range-and-volume set-up occurred and the stock made a rapid excursion above the consolidation range. The AGP expansion-of-range-and-volume move, when examined in this context, becomes a very attractive trading candidate.

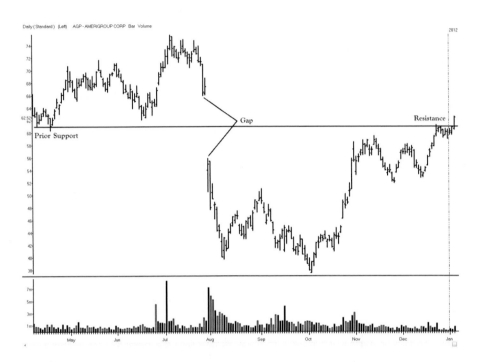

FIGURE 4.2 – AMERIGROUP CORPORATION (II)
RealTick by Townsend Analytics, Ltd.

Drilling down on a five-minute chart (Figure 4.3) of the expansion-of-range-and-volume set-up day reveals that AGP closed in the top of its range and attracted significant institutional interest in doing so. Volume was very heavy going into the final minutes of trading, indicating to me that buyers were probably unable to finish their accumulation of the stock. This push into the close tells me that, if accumulation resumes in the morning, AGP will most likely move higher to the next level of daily resistance.

FIGURE 4.3 – AMERIGROUP CORPORATION (III)
RealTick by Townsend Analytics, Ltd.

All of the factors presented in the examination of AGP represent pieces of a puzzle that I put together to form my trading plan. I will present several more examples and then demonstrate how to structure a trading plan based on the price action in the examples.

Harley Davidson Inc.

Another good example occurred in Harley Davidson Inc. (HOG). The stock generated two expansion-of-range-and-volume entries over the course of two weeks, both of them subsequent to consolidations. Notice in Figure 4.4 that daily volume in both cases was again above the average volume during the consolidation periods. The consolidation ranges developed after an upward move in the price of HOG, and the stock's price behaviour meets the basic criterion for the expansion-of-range-and-volume set-up very well.

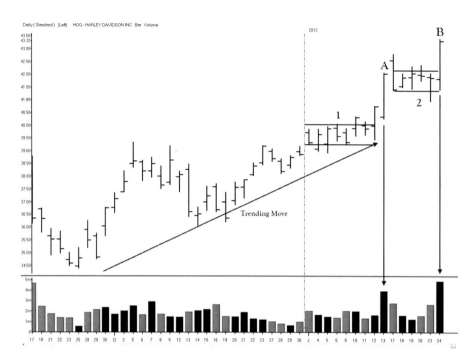

Trending Move

FIGURE 4.4 – HARLEY DAVIDSON INC. (I)
RealTick by Townsend Analytics, Ltd.

As was the case with AGP, the back story on HOG provides further insight into the strength of the set-up. We see in Figure 4.5 that in, July 2011, HOG gapped significantly higher after reporting second-quarter profits of more than $190 million. That was up from $71 million the prior year, and beat expectations by more than $20 million. The stock then traded in a distribution-consolidation range, as investors locked in profits and began selling the stock. The selling matured into a mark-down phase which saw HOG lose 30% of its value. This was followed by an entire quarter of what I definitely interpreted as bad volatility. There were no solid trading set-ups in HOG for nearly four months and the volatility also served as a de facto accumulation range. The ensuing mark-up ultimately led to the expansion-of-range-and-volume set-ups in Figure 4.4. A close look at price in the January 2012 reveals that the expansion-of-range-and-volume set-ups that HOG generated were challenging the June and July 2011 levels of support and resistance. This ensures logical placement of profit objectives, and also suggests that players will be drawn back into the market as price moves higher. Previous areas of exaggerated price and volume activity generally are indicative of similar activity in the future, should price reach the same levels.

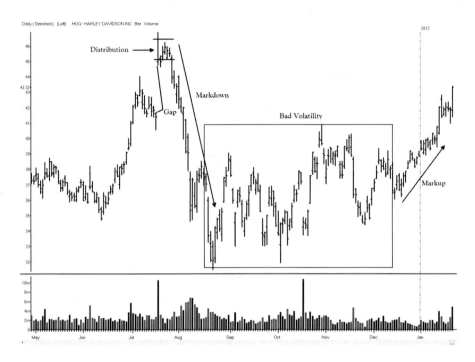

FIGURE 4.5 – HARLEY DAVIDSON INC. (II)
RealTick by Townsend Analytics, Ltd.

The five-minute chart of the second expansion-of-range-and-volume set-up in this example (Figure 4.6) shows increased price and volume momentum in the first hour and last hour of the trading session. Interest in buying the stock occurred on heavy volume in the session. Buyers were unable to overcome the hurdle established by the strong open, as HOG trended higher throughout the trading day. A close look at the ticker tape reveals that many prints are on sizeable volume. This elevates the probability of continued buying on a strong broader open, and increases the likelihood of a successful trade.

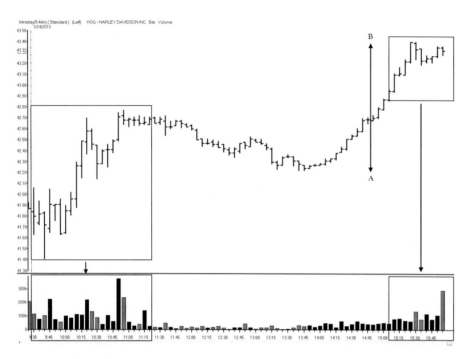

FIGURE 4.6 – HARLEY DAVIDSON INC. (III)
RealTick by Townsend Analytics, Ltd.

Finally, the HOG example shows the utility of using measured moves as a way to gauge the prospects for profits in an intraday position when a stock is moving in the 'push, pause, push again' trending momentum that is seen on expansion days. If I see such a pattern form on the set-up day, my strategy is to measure the thrust and use approximately 80% of that range, in conjunction with daily support and resistance, to establish targets on the planned trade for the next session. In Figure 4.6, the dollar value of the move from point A to point B is $1.18. This overlaps with the low of the day after the bar that created the July 2011 gap in Figure 4.5. The overlap suggests a good point of confluence to use as a first target on the trade. The utility of measured moves in projecting price does not end there. As figure 4.7 demonstrates, when additional intraday entry or extension opportunities are available, the value of the measured move can be used for significant additional profits.

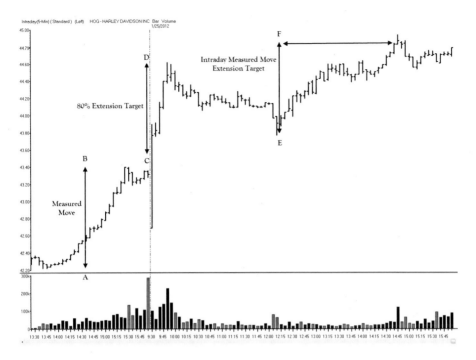

FIGURE 4.7 – HARLEY DAVIDSON INC. (IV)
RealTick by Townsend Analytics, Ltd.

The first move, from point A to point B, is used to develop the expansion-of-range-and-volume initial profit target for the trigger day. When HOG achieves the profit target, the resistance caused by investors who are still holding the stock from the gap day in Figure 4.5 generates a mild sell-off. This is to be expected, as many investors and traders witnessed the 30% collapse in the stock the previous year from this level. They understandably do not wish to be part of a repeat performance, and will take profits when the C–D move develops. The resulting move lower finds support. When HOG attempts to break below that support, a continuation entry opportunity presents itself as heavy volume pushes the stock back into the range. A thrust above the range high triggers an entry, with a profit target at the E–F repeat of the C–D measured move.

I know many traders who have tried to extend this logic into the following session. They assume that an extension target of approximately the magnitude of the set-up day's measured moves is a reasonable expectation. I have found, however, that a move to nearby support and resistance in a daily and weekly time frame is much more realistic and will provide the logic for developing targets in the next chapter.

Summary

I have covered how to find the most promising expansion-of-range-and-volume set-ups. This is the first step of the planning process. To consistently succeed in the markets, a trader should view the market as a puzzle that needs to be approached with a coherent and logical plan. The next step in the planning process is to anticipate and plan for adverse price moves. Then a trader needs to develop a logical means of pinpointing price zones that will likely represent maximum profitability on a trade. Finally, traders need to find a way to tighten up trailing stops behind a profitable position. I will cover these three procedures in the next chapter.

CHAPTER 5.
Setting Stops and Profit Targets

TRADERS WHO HOPE to keep a trading business viable will definitely need to intimately acquaint themselves with the notion of natural support and resistance and the role it plays in defining the parameters of their trading activities. Over the years, I have taught thousands of people how to trade. In many cases, I am able to predict who will not be in business long based entirely on the context of a single conversation. It usually goes something like this:

ADRIAN: So tell me a little about how you are defining your acceptable risk on any given trade.

TRADER: It's pretty straightforward. I never risk more than two per cent of my account on a single position.

ADRIAN: So you adjust your position size constantly to account for the risk you will accept?

TRADER: No. I adjust the amount of the stop and trade my usual lot size. I know what I am comfortable losing, and that's where I draw the line.

ADRIAN: Well, what makes you think that the market cares how much you are comfortable losing?

TRADER: . . . I guess I never thought of it that way.

Luckily, there is a simple remedy to this common ailment. I set logical stops and targets based on natural support and resistance. I do this for every trade I am considering, and ultimately the presence of a reasonable stop and a readily definable target determine whether or not a potential trade will wind up in my *Around The Horn Trading Plan*.

Remember that when I write 'logical' what I am referring to is an area based on natural support and resistance. There are other legitimate price zones that can be used to refine targets and stops, and I add them as secondary sources of confirmation when developing my trading plan. Fibonacci retracement levels, for example, are almost always in the back of my mind when I look at any pattern in a trend. The 38.2% and 50% retracements and extensions have proven particularly reliable, but only when accompanied by underlying natural support and resistance. I use them when I see a clear trend on the intraday and daily charts. The more overlap there is between the factors I consider, the more credence I give to their ability to impact my trade.

I also use floor trader pivots as a means of anticipating likely areas of support and resistance in planning an upcoming trade. Pivots tend to be self-fulfilling prophecies in terms of intraday inflection points. I am certain to incorporate their effect into my rationale when trying to figure out the ease of movement a stock will experience when I enter a trade. The formulas are developed for tomorrow's trading based on today's daily bar price action and are presented in Figure 5.1.

The central pivot	$P = (high + low + close) \div 3$
First resistance	$R1 = 2 \times P - low$
First support	$S1 = 2 \times P - high$
Second resistance	$R2 = P + (R1 - S1)$
Second support	$S2 = P - (R1 - S1)$

FIGURE 5.1 – PIVOT CALCULATIONS

Finally, I use volume-weighted average price (VWAP) as a validation tool for developing intraday stops. VWAP is calculated by adding up the dollars traded for every transaction during a specified time period (price × share volume traded) and then dividing by the total shares traded for the period being observed. Most people think of the VWAP as a tool for longer-term portfolio allocation, but, when considering intraday price data, the equation does a nice job of identifying where support and resistance may lie based on trading activity that may not be readily apparent just by looking at price data on a chart. The calculation for the VWAP is presented in Figure 5.2.

$$VWAP = \frac{\Sigma \text{ number of shares} \times \text{price per share}}{\text{Total shares transacted during period}}$$

FIGURE 5.2 – VOLUME WEIGHTED AVERAGE PRICE FORMULA

I will be using examples from my trading plan as I illustrate the placement of logical stops and targets. At the end of this section, readers should have a good idea of how to set targets and stops.

KBR Inc

KBR Inc (KBR) demonstrates the utility of all the target and stop concepts discussed so far. A look at the charts shows the following:

On the five-minute chart (Figure 5.3), notice that the closing range has a significant volume spike and that the session downtrend is persistent. As KBR moves lower, attempted pullbacks reverse and the trend reasserts itself. As the day progresses, natural support and resistance is evident in five regions on the chart. These are all areas that could hinder upside price action the following day.

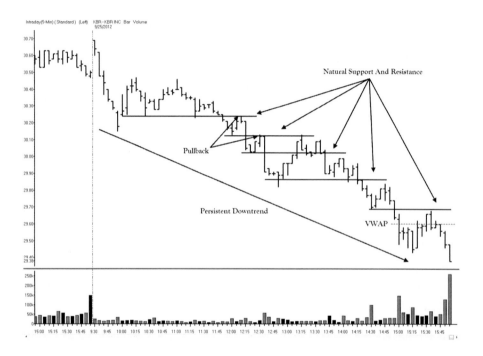

FIGURE 5.3 – KBR INC (I)
RealTick by Townsend Analytics, Ltd.

Ultimately, a decision needs to be made, and this is where the VWAP is useful. The VWAP shows where most trading actually took place and at what price level natural support and resistance is most significant. In the KBR example, the VWAP provides a tighter stop than the lowest natural support and resistance line, and actually defines another, untested resistance zone. In order for price to reach the $29.70

price level of the last natural support and resistance line, it will first have to penetrate the VWAP of the final leg of KBR's move lower. This represents confluence between the VWAP and the final support. The final support and resistance level at $29.70 gives the KBR expansion-of-range-and-volume set-up a little bit more room to travel so it is a logical stop.

The daily chart (Figure 5.4) shows well-defined levels of support over the previous 12 months. Ownership decisions of KBR occur around the $29.00–$34.00 level, frequently on heavy volume. The presence of previous reaction moves at a specific price is indicative of future reaction moves at the same price, in the same time frame. I definitely do not want to get caught in an updraft if price reverses there again, so my target on the day trade is at $28.77, which keeps me above the most recent reaction area, and I hope will allow me to take profits before significant buying pressure affects KBR.

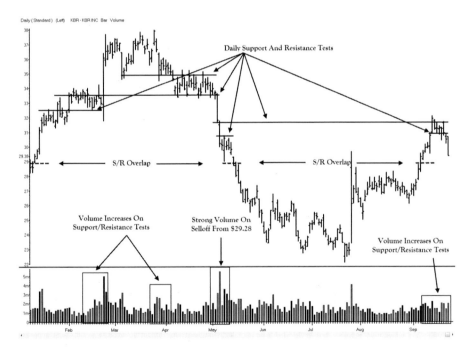

FIGURE 5.4 – KBR INC (II)
RealTick by Townsend Analytics, Ltd.

Figure 5.5 is the weekly chart of KBR. The support and resistance identified on the daily chart is confirmed in the weekly time compression. Even more evidence exists that the target price on the trade is logical, and will likely be a short-term inflection zone.

With the entry at $29.28, the stop loss at $29.70 and the target at $28.77, the potential loss on the trade is $0.42 and the initial profit potential is $0.51. The profit-to-loss ratio on the set-up is 1.21:1. I take trades only with better than 1:1 profit to loss ratios.

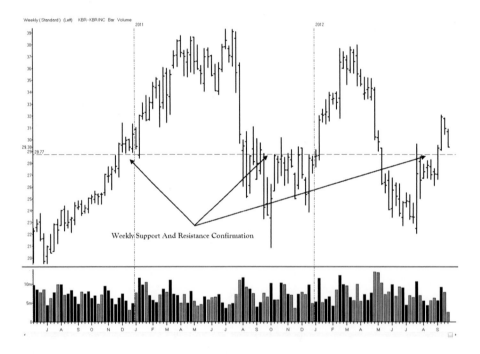

FIGURE 5.5 – KBR INC (III)
RealTick by Townsend Analytics, Ltd.

On page 48 is the actual KBR set-up as it appeared in my *Around The Horn Trading Plan* for 26 September 2012. Notice the level of specificity I use in planning every one of my trades. I do not like to leave much open to interpretation during the trading session. My analysis is all conducted the day before a trade will take place, and all the levels that will be important once a trade has triggered are clearly established in my plan. I identify all the necessary trade parameters (entry, stop, 50% to target, and target). I also make note of each potential pivot inflection and identify the sector with which the stock is most highly correlated.

What is the purpose of the 50% level and the sector correlation? Fifty per cent to the profit target represents an expansion range that is also a Fibonacci ratio. It tends to be a make-or-break zone for a live trade, and I use it as a means of ratcheting stops once a position is established. If I make it from the entry price to the 50%-to-target level, I move my stop on the position to break-even. If the price reverses from the 50% level and returns to the entry, I will close out the position at break-even. I will re-enter the trade if it moves through the entry price and triggers me back in again. Over time, this strategy has served me well by exiting a trade before a major reversal would have taken me to the planned stop loss

The sector symbol that I include on the trading plan is something that newer traders often ask me about. Price action does not happen in a vacuum. And while it is true that I execute my trading plan more or less robotically during the session, there are times when a little discretionary decision-making ability is a good thing. One is the situation in which the stock opens strongly against my anticipated trade. The other is when a trade moves to the profit target and then continues decisively through it.

On a given day, I might have a strong short-side bias in my trading plan, but the market and my stocks gap higher. Depending on what caused the gap and if my trading-plan stocks happen to be trading at a pivot or natural overhead resistance level, I will start looking for opportunities to enter positions early on a broader reversal. The deciding factor for shorting stocks earlier than planned is whether or not the sectors to which the stocks' price action is most highly correlated is leading the move lower. Price action begets price action, and a move in the broader markets followed by a move in the sectors is generally followed by a strong move in individual stocks. So keeping an eye on the sector within which a stock trades can create an early entry and substantial profit opportunity.

The second use for sector data is in determining whether or not to let profits run once the profit target is hit. If my planned trade results in a move to the profit target and the price moves decisively through the established objective, my first action is to look at the sector. If the sector action shows signs of slowing down, I will close a portion of the position and trail tightly on the balance at the original target. If the sector price action is accelerating in my favour, I will keep the entire trade open and trail stops at the reversal of two five-minute closing prices. If price pops back to the initial profit target, I will exit the entire position.

Now I will work through the KBR example in detail. I will start by presenting the actual plan for the trade from my daily service. Then I will describe what happened on the trigger day on a five-minute chart.

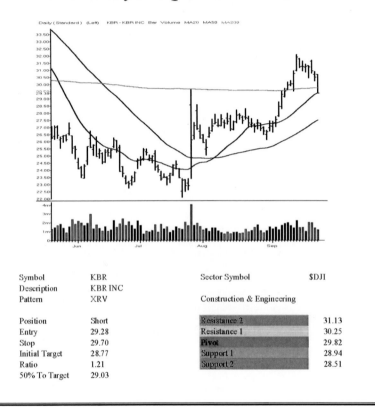

Around The Horn Plan
Wednesday, September 26, 2012

Symbol	KBR	Sector Symbol	$DJI
Description	KBR INC		
Pattern	XRV	Construction & Engineering	

Position	Short	Resistance 2	31.13
Entry	29.28	Resistance 1	30.25
Stop	29.70	Pivot	29.82
Initial Target	28.77	Support 1	28.94
Ratio	1.21	Support 2	28.51
50% To Target	29.03		

KBR PLAN

Figure 5.6 shows the result of the KBR set-up on the day of the intraday trade. The stock opened and immediately began moving higher. It tested a price level near the stop loss and reversed lower. This behaviour gave me additional confidence in the set-up, as a level of resistance at the stop had been confirmed. The stop loss also halted price prior to a test of the central pivot, giving additional credibility to the choice of $29.70 as a point to exit the trade on a counter-position move after an entry. If the price had traded at the central pivot, I would have immediately looked to the sector for signs of a reversal and considered an early entry on sector price confirmation. KBR did not provide the extra profit opportunity, but did trigger an entry on a decline just moments later. The stock moved to the 50%-to-target level, prompting me to move the stop to break-even. At this point, if KBR traded back to the entry price I would have closed out the position for no gain or loss. One half hour into the session, KBR hit the profit target, prompting an exit. KBR proceeded to rebound to the S1 Pivot. After testing price elasticity at S1, the stock reversed and moved lower to the S2 level.

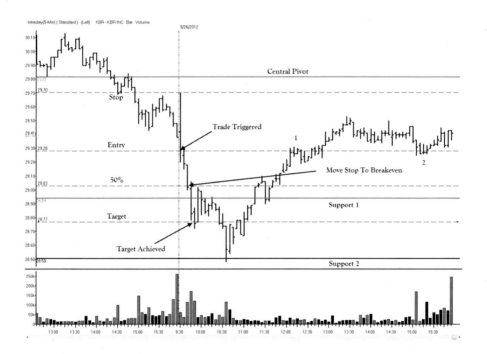

FIGURE 5.6 – KBR INC (IV)
RealTick by Townsend Analytics, Ltd.

A midday retest of the entry (1) price did not qualify for a second entry, as I require price to move a minimum of $0.08 above the short-sale price to qualify a new position. KBR did make the required excursion above the entry later in the session, and a second entry (2) resulted in an exit with a minor $0.07 loss. The total net for the position was thus a gain of $0.44 per share traded (+$0.51 on the first position, -$0.07 on the second).

This example should also make evident the importance of meticulous planning. No guesswork was involved in the execution of the trade. Every contingency was planned for, and I knew exactly what to do at every step of the way.

Iamgold Corp

In the case of Iamgold Corp (IAG), notice the following.

1. Looking at the daily and weekly charts (Figure 5.8 and Figure 5.9), there was clear resistance for the proposed long position at $14.84. This area had been natural support and resistance on many occasions over the past two years, and was a logical area to expect price to pause if it moved swiftly in my favour. This defined $14.84 (strong and frequent previous support and resistance) as a logical profit objective.

2. The trading plan page shows that the potential loss on the trade was $0.27 per share and that the initial profit potential was $0.43 per share. The profit-to-loss ratio on the set-up was 1.59:1, making this a trade set-up to include in my trading plan.

3. On the five-minute chart (Figure 5.7), the day's trading started on moderate volume. Price and volume spiked sharply higher after economic news favourable to IAG was released. The closing range had a significant spike in volume, but the resistance at the top of the range remained well defined. This tells me that if overhead supply is exhausted early in the following trading session, a sharp move higher may occur. The move would likely continue until the next level of daily resistance, which will again represent an area of substantial supply. The bottom of the trading range represents natural support, and the VWAP of the price expansion move that started with the economic news report is higher than natural support, indicating a double hurdle and giving me a high level of confidence in the support-based stop loss.

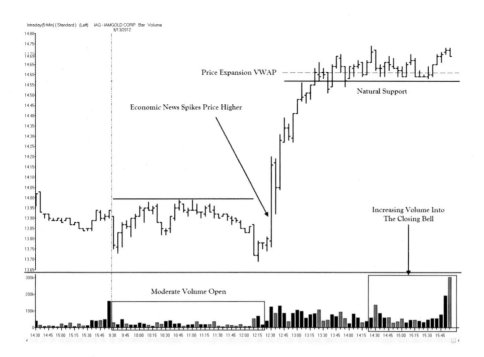

FIGURE 5.7 – IAMGOLD CORP (I)
RealTick by Townsend Analytics, Ltd.

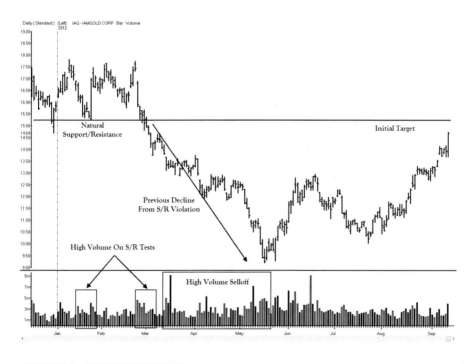

FIGURE 5.8 – IAMGOLD CORP (II)
RealTick by Townsend Analytics, Ltd.

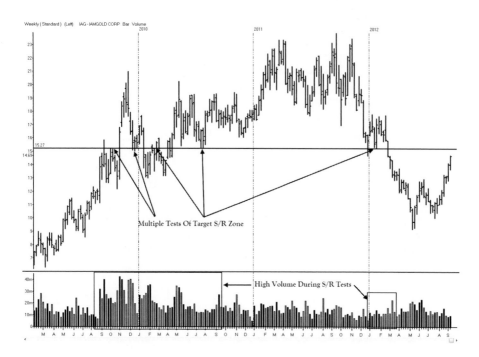

Multiple Tests Of Target S/R Zone

High Volume During S/R Tests

FIGURE 5.9 – IAMGOLD CORP (III)
RealTick by Townsend Analytics, Ltd.

By placing my protective stops and targets around natural support and resistance, I ensure that I am on the same side of the price action. Honouring my profit-to-loss ratio requirements ensures that the risks I am taking in my trading business will make sense and that I will survive long term. Page 54 shows the actual IAG set-up from my *Around The Horn Trading Plan.*

Figure 5.10 is a five-minute intraday chart of the trade, which triggered on 15 September 2012. Notice that the stock opened a few cents above the planned entry, triggering a long position right at the opening bell. The move from the entry to the initial profit target occurred in the first ten minutes (two five-minute bars) of trading and represented a measured move. The support/resistance that developed just above the target a few minutes later further reinforced the usefulness of the measured move for later trading.

Later in the session, IAG traded smoothly through resistance 2 (R2) and found support. An entry just above R2 with a stop at the support/resistance that developed earlier in the day (R2 violation entry stop), and a profit target at a measured move extension yielded a profit-to-loss ratio of better than 2:1, making the pivot entry very attractive. The combined effect of the two entries was a $0.85-per-share profit.

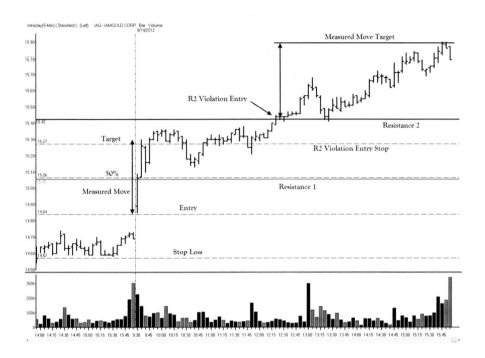

FIGURE 5.10 – IAMGOLD CORP (IV)
RealTick by Townsend Analytics, Ltd.

Around The Horn Plan
Friday, September 14, 2012

Symbol	IAG	Sector Symbol	$XAU.X
Description	IAMGOLD CORP		
Pattern	XRV	Gold	

Position	Long	Resistance 2	15.42
Entry	14.84	Resistance 1	15.06
Stop	14.57	Pivot	14.37
Initial Target	15.27	Support 1	14.01
Ratio	1.59	Support 2	13.32
50% To Target	15.06		

IAG PLAN

Harman International Industries

Finally, Harman International Industries (HAR) provides another good example of how to properly plan and execute an expansion-of-range-and-volume trade. The following are the noteworthy characteristics HAR exhibited in each time frame:

1. On the five-minute chart (Figure 5.11), HAR makes a steady trending move on the set-up day. Over the course of the first three hours of trading, the stock climbs its trend line in an orderly fashion, making predictable pullback moves

along the way. A volume surge into the closing minutes of trading is indicative of institutional interest in HAR, and for the potential for follow-through in the morning. Natural support and resistance develop later in the session at $47.26, just below the VWAP for the final leg of the move, which is at $47.35. The confluence of the two values gives me confidence in my planned stop of $47.26.

2. Daily resistance is easy to spot in Figure 5.12 at $48.23, as price has turned at this level on several occasions, and has done so on heavy volume.

3. Figure 5.13 shows that the same support and resistance inflection is evident in the trading of HAR all the way back to 2010. $47.26 becomes the initial profit target for my 7 September 2012 trading plan which can be found on page 58. As is always the case with a planned trade, the ratio of reward to risk at 1.26:1 represents an acceptable risk profile for the set-up.

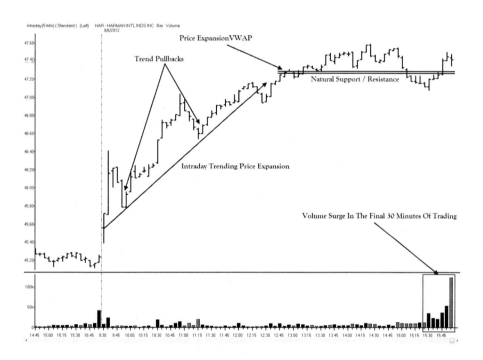

FIGURE 5.11 – HARMAN INTERNATIONAL INDUSTRIES (I)
RealTick by Townsend Analytics, Ltd.

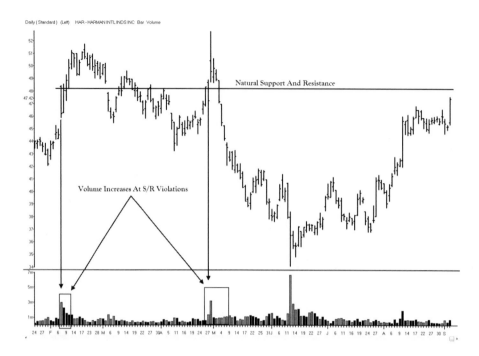

FIGURE 5.12 – HARMAN INTERNATIONAL INDUSTRIES (II)
RealTick by Townsend Analytics, Ltd.

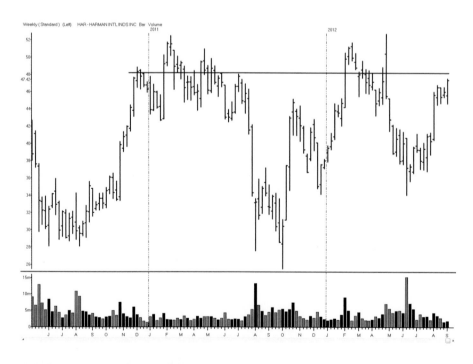

FIGURE 5.13 – HARMAN INTERNATIONAL INDUSTRIES (III)
RealTick by Townsend Analytics, Ltd.

Figure 5.14 shows the price action on the day that the HAR trade triggered an entry. The stock hit the entry price within a few minutes of the open, then immediately traded to the 50% to target level. At this point, I moved my stop loss to the break-even (entry) level. Two minutes later, I was stopped out at the $47.69 entry price, only to be triggered back into the HAR trade within five minutes. The stock then traveled to the 50% mark again, reversed course and almost stopped out, only to reverse again and move to the profit target. The efficacy of the support and resistance target methodology is seen here again, as the $48.23 multiple-time frame-confluence target was the exact high of the session.

FIGURE 5.14 – HARMAN INTERNATIONAL INDUSTRIES (IV)
RealTick by Townsend Analytics, Ltd.

By placing my protective stops and targets around natural support and resistance, I ensure that I am on the same side of the price action. Honouring my profit-to-loss ratio requirements ensures that the risks I am taking in my trading business will make sense and I will survive long term.

Around The Horn Plan
Friday, September 07, 2012

Symbol	HAR	Sector Symbol	$IXY.X
Description	HARMAN INTL INDS INC		
Pattern	XRV	Consumer Electronics	

Position	Long	Resistance 2	49.00
Entry	47.69	Resistance 1	48.21
Stop	47.26	Pivot	46.80
Initial Target	48.23	Support 1	46.01
Ratio	1.26	Support 2	44.60
50% To Target	47.96		

HAR PLAN

Summary

The daily expansion-of-range-and-volume set-up is a bread-and-butter trade that can provide excellent income opportunities for the disciplined intraday trader. The key is staying focused and following the trading plan to the letter. The planning process involves far more than determining that a particular stock looks appealing for a particular trading session. A good plan identifies every contingency and puts the trader in the powerful position of knowing exactly what to do and when to do it. This frees up significant time to find developing real-time opportunities, such as the news expansion set-ups that I discuss in the next chapter.

CHAPTER 6.
Day Trading News Events

A NYONE WHO SITS in front of a trading workstation all day knows that opportunity is not always easy to find. While finding intraday set-ups can be a simple matter of running pattern-scanning software, it is not easy to filter the good from the bad. Lack of time to evaluate candidates usually results in a failure to plan the trade and a random execution with no idea of where to expect price to go. I believe that the absence of careful planning is the primary reason so many traders blow out their accounts.

One solution is to find trades that essentially set themselves up. The implementation of the expansion-of-range-and-volume set-up that I will show here does that. It serves to present a manageable number of intraday trading candidates as opposed to churning out countless set-ups of questionable merit over the course of the day. I should emphasise now that this is definitely not a strategy for anyone using a web-based broker. Without a direct access trading platform, this or any other scalping strategy is impossible to implement profitably. This is also not a strategy for beginners. Traders should be very comfortable analysing intraday charts and reading the ticker tape in real time if they are looking to add this or any other intraday strategy to their repertoire.

Trading News

A typical trading day is filled with many news events. Economic announcements, earnings reports, SEC filings, and breaking news on the major networks are the sources that most traders follow. They are also all in a category of information that will do nothing for traders unless there is a major surprise in what is being reported. Many of these events are scheduled to occur before or after market hours, which further limits their utility. The impact of surprising pre- and post-market news is generally to gap the market open the next time that trading commences. Since most traders trade only during normal New York session hours, the influence of pre- and post-market news is immaterial when it comes to the bottom line.

Let's say, for example, that the US Labor Department is going to release employment numbers and that Wall Street is expecting 600,000 new jobs to have been created. When the news is announced an hour before the market opens, it turns out that 350,000 jobs were actually lost. This would shock the overnight futures market and probably create a substantial gap lower on the New York market open. But the reaction of the market after the gap lower is hard to anticipate and very tricky to trade. Since the news has already impacted the market in the overnight futures trade, there is little one can do to find opportunity in the announcement. Bad volatility will engulf the opening price action and, more often than not, trades that are made with risk control in place will get stopped out for a loss as the market swings higher and lower while traders try to make sense of the uncertainty.

As for news reports issued on television, my advice is to forget them. While it may sometimes be entertaining to listen as the talking heads bicker about politics, there is seldom anything reported on any of the cable or satellite financial news channels that will provide actionable information. Broadcasts are written by writers, edited by editors, and scheduled by producers. The more significant the news, the more likely it will be fully reported after a commercial break. For the purposes of the typical intraday trader, this news has now become useless. I do have a television in my office. But if it is on at all, it is tuned to Bloomberg and is muted. That way if something catastrophic is unfolding somewhere, I will be aware of it. Otherwise, I turn up the volume only if I see an interesting report on one of the European exchanges.

As for newspapers, I read the *Wall Street Journal* and *Financial Times* (UK edition) on my tablet every day at the gym. They provide nothing in terms of actionable information, but they do keep me informed of what is happening in the financial markets around the world, and the content provides a useful backdrop for my work.

Where can one find news that provides actionable information? In my case, I monitor multiple financial wire services. These services are the sources for many of the stories that will be picked up later by the mainstream media, and give me a head start in evaluating the potential impact an event will have on a market.

Among the high quality wire services that are available, *Trade The News* and *The Fly on the Wall* are my favourites (**tradethenews.com**, **theflyonthewall.com**), with audio and text alerts that are announced seconds and sometimes minutes before most other vendors report an event. This gives me time to pull up the five-minute bar chart and evaluate what is happening rather than just to react to every broadcast. Among the many categories of events that are reported every day, I find that takeover chatter is the most likely piece of news to drive an intraday expansion-of-range-and-volume set-up.

There are usually a few takeover rumours circulating every day, but not all of them form tradeable patterns. Patiently looking at the charts after every announcement will lead to multiple solid candidates every week. Trading them definitely requires some skill and finesse, as the expansion-of-range-and-volume rules need to be slightly bent in order for the set-ups to make sense. As I will show later, there is opportunity available with news-driven set-ups in waiting for and trading the counter-expansion move, which is generally on the short side of the market.

I want to focus first on what the expectation should be with an expansion strategy applied to the intraday time compression. These are basically scalp set-ups, and scalping involves looking for small, fast moves that can add .10–.40 per share profit within a few minutes. Scalping requires thinking on the fly and a willingness to close out losses very quickly. One loss that is allowed to run can wipe out the gains achieved by many successful positions. Remember that traders looking for .10–.20 per share in profit are usually trading in very large numbers of shares. When a trade goes wrong, even a small loss per share can greatly impact the account as a whole.

When I trade in anticipation of a .10-.20 per share gain, for example, my lot size will be 2,000–5,000 shares depending on the liquidity of the stock I am trading. I assess the liquidity by evaluating the activity on a 25-tick chart or on the time-of-sales ticker tape. If the number of shares I would like to trade cannot typically be transacted in just a few ticks, I will move on to another set-up. If I see adequate liquidity to get in and out of the market with a lot size at least as large as what I want to trade, I will take an entry with a stop loss placed at support or resistance on a 25-tick chart. These scalps are typically the toughest way to do business, but if a trader is comfortable executing them and has the discipline to follow the rules, the profits can be substantial over time. As an ancillary strategy, scalping is terrific, but I recommend that traders buy lots of antacids if the goal is to trade primarily this type of price action. Scalping as a primary strategy is a very stressful approach to the markets and, as far as I am concerned, there are many easier ways to earn a living trading.

Setting up an expansion-of-range-and-volume trade intraday requires cognitive flexibility. Remember that on a daily or weekly chart, traders are evaluating significant amounts of closing data to find pattern set-ups. Planning intraday trades from intraday charts is far more subjective than looking for the same set-ups in the daily time compression. Intraday, the time compression chosen by traders can be arbitrary. I like five-minute charts, though I have friends who trade from one-minute, three-minute, 15-minute and 60-minute charts. Thinking about it for a second, it should be evident that bar compression is going to make a difference in how various traders would evaluate the same set of data. Essentially, looking for moves intraday dictates finding patterns that are in the spirit of the set-up, even though they may not form consolidations or pullbacks with the same precision that their counterparts on a daily chart do.

The rules for the set-up need to be adjusted to take all of this into account. Generally speaking, my rules for the entry and targeting of profits are as follows:

1. After a takeover chatter news event, range and volume expand when compared to a typical price bar in the same time compression. Noisy intraday data precludes using a 10-bar lookback as a filter, so I eyeball the chart and make a quick assessment of what is typical.

2. The stock starts trading much more frequently and with much more sell-side activity than had been the case earlier in the session.

3. Price may retrace into the body of the range expansion bar, and can extend into several additional inside price bars, or move higher (for longs) immediately after the expansion bar is in place. Entry is on just a few cents of confirmation above the expansion bar, and the target is based on an expansion to a pivot, natural resistance, a measured move, or the 150% Fibonacci extension of the expansion bar.

Some examples of the pattern for the intraday set-up follow.

Onyx Pharmaceuticals Inc

When an industry is frequently in the news, the big players in the group tend to see a great deal of reaction trading. Onyx Pharmaceuticals Inc (ONXX) is often the subject of rumours, as the pharmaceutical sector tends to generate a great deal of news and speculation about new products and corporate buyouts. On 25 April 2012 (Figure 6.1), takeover chatter was circulating. A few moments after the first announcement, I saw an expansion-of-range-and-volume set-up. The entry level was a few cents above the high of the bar that created the pattern, and the target was a measured-expansion move.

After the trade triggered, ONXX quickly reached the measured-move extension target. The price action had minimal bleed back as ONXX moved higher on increasing volume. Achieving the target had closed the trade, but another entry opportunity was soon available, as ONXX made an orderly pullback, followed by another thrust higher. The target for the second entry was the high of the first extension move after the news release. ONXX made several additional extension moves, but without a clear rationale for entry, I chose to pass on another entry.

I always get questions about leaving profits on the table, and my answer is always the same. Every trade needs to be accompanied by an objective set of rules. This is the only way to evaluate a trading methodology. In the case of intraday scalps, performance evaluation is based on a set of rules constructed to capture fast, small profits. What a trade did after a plan was executed is of no consequence. I am interested only in my ability to carry out my strategies according to the rules.

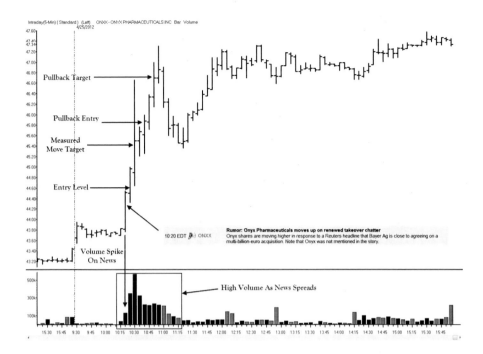

Intraday(5-Min) (Standard) (Left)   ONXX - ONYX PHARMACEUTICALS INC Bar Volume
4/25/2012

Pullback Target

Pullback Entry

Measured
Move Target

Entry Level

Volume Spike
On News

10:20 EDT 📂 ONXX

Rumor: Onyx Pharmaceuticals moves up on renewed takeover chatter
Onyx shares are moving higher in response to a Reuters headline that Bayer Ag is close to agreeing on a
multi-billion-euro acquisition. Note that Onyx was not mentioned in the story.

High Volume As News Spreads

FIGURE 6.1 – ONYX PHARMACEUTICALS INC
RealTick by Townsend Analytics, Ltd.

Nu Skin Enterprises Inc

When investors hear that a 'China strategy' is in the works for a company, they tend to become interested very quickly. China represents opportunity on many levels, and early investment can be the key to profitability. Once China news starts circulating, stocks can make exaggerated moves on even the smallest bit of information, as was the case when news began appearing on the wires which indicated that Nu Skin Enterprises Inc (NUS) five-year business development plan for mainland China might not be as attractive as it was originally thought to be by analysts.

In Figure 6.2, we see an intraday expansion-of-range-and-volume set-up appear as rumours begin circulating. The thrust lower sets up a $36.99 short sale, with a measured-move target of $36.59. NUS triggers the entry, makes a violent move lower to the target, and immediately retraces to the entry price on heavy volume.

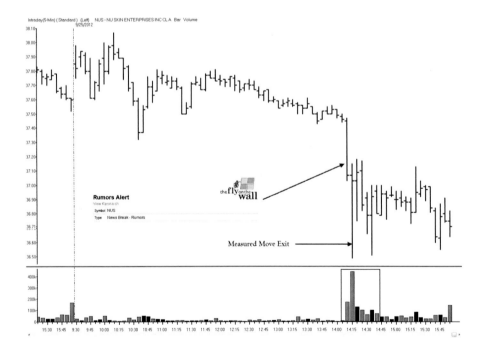

FIGURE 6.2 – NU SKIN ENTERPRISES INC
RealTick by Townsend Analytics, Ltd.

Monster Beverage Corp.

Determining the stop on the intraday trade is readily accomplished using a 25-tick chart. Support and resistance in a 25-tick compression will essentially yield a price zone that represents where most of the volume in the expansion bar occurred. Many trading platforms do not offer 25-tick compression, and an alternative to finding the support and resistance directly is to reduce the chart to its minimum compression in minutes and find a VWAP for the area that created the expansion. The Monster Beverage Corp. (MNST) example in Figure 6.3 shows the utility of such a stop. In this case, the probability of a measured-move extension was mitigated by an overhead R1 pivot, and when price reversed, the Expansion-VWAP protective stop managed to keep the MNST trade from becoming a loser.

The MNST intraday entry was at $60.99, after renewed takeover chatter prompted high levels of option trading activity. The VWAP during the expansion bars was $61.05, and the R2 pivot was at $61.13. MNST turned lower well below my $61.56 measured-move target, and when the VWAP was violated, it was time to close the position. Note that the VWAP for protective stops should be calculated from the expansion-of-range-and-volume bar to the final bar that makes a new high. This ensures that the VWAP is representative of the period of time in which price momentum was supporting the direction of the position.

If all of that sounds a bit convoluted for a decision that has to be made on the fly, rest assured that after many trades have flashed on the screen, the measured-move target will pop out without needing a Fibonacci drawing tool. That leaves only the quick plot of the VWAP (for those without 25-tick charting) in order to properly set up the plan for the trade. The VWAP tool is available in most charting software under the line-drawing tools. Many packages also allow traders to calculate the value automatically in the *time of sales* window.

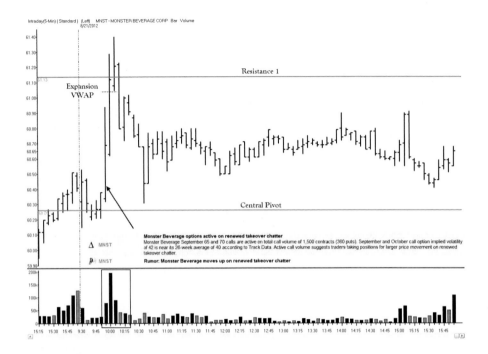

FIGURE 6.3 – MONSTER BEVERAGE CORP.
RealTick by Townsend Analytics, Ltd.

Walter Energy Inc

While measured moves are a great way to project targets, pivot-to-pivot projections are often easier to work with since they are automatically calculated and plotted. They can also be more reliable as predictors of potential inflections than just about any indicator except for natural support and resistance, as they represent price points that will be watched by legions of traders. The Walter Energy Inc (WLT) example in Figure 6.4 illustrates the point nicely.

Renewed takeover chatter at 09:45 started an expansion-of-range-and-volume move in WLT. The stock penetrated the central pivot and triggered an entry at $61.30. WLT moved rapidly higher, and traveled through R1, further extending gains. A rapid reversal triggered an exit at $61.84, just below R1, and WLT retraced all the way to the entry price before making another move higher. A second entry opportunity occurred when WLT made another expansion-of-range-and-volume move just a few minutes later. This time, the breakout above the high of the first measured move at \$62.25 was the entry trigger, and the target was at \$63.06, the level plotted in Figure 6.4 as R2.

Using pivot lines as price projections is a very useful technique, particularly when a long or short move starts at the central pivot and there is sufficient room between pivots for acceptable profitability. A review of the pivot line calculations (page 42) shows that greater travel range between pivots is most readily found in stocks that normally trade in a wide range. This is a function of the fact that the central pivot, from which the other pivot lines are derived, is calculated as an average of the previous session's high, low and close. If the high and low are not separated by sufficient travel range, then the following session's pivots will have less distance between them, and will not be useful in planning targets.

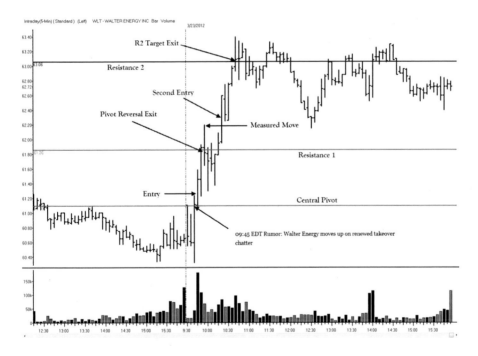

FIGURE 6.4 – WALTER ENERGY INC
RealTick by Townsend Analytics, Ltd.

Mosaic Corporation

Mosaic Corporation (MOS) is a member of the volatile specialty chemical sector. The company is a potash producer and is very frequently in the news, making it a favourite of traders who are stalking volatility set-ups. MOS tends to inflect at intraday pivot lines, and most traders who follow the stock would be very comfortable working under the assumption that an expansion-of-range-and-volume move would be likely to inflect at a pivot line, even if only momentarily.

In Figure 6.5 MOS triggers an intraday entry after takeover chatter led to an expansion-of-range-and-volume move. The measured-move target and the pivot target are almost identical, and this confluence provides additional rationale for using an exit at the first sign of a reversal at R1. Over the course of ten minutes, MOS made a volatile move that resulted in a gain of $0.36 per share.

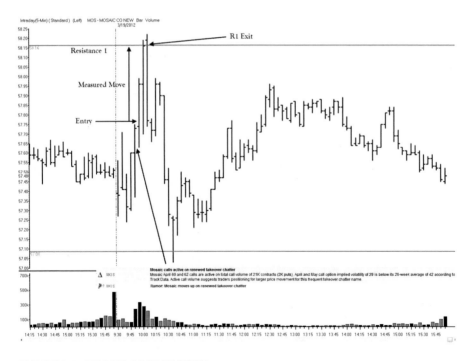

FIGURE 6.5 – MOSAIC CORPORATION
RealTick by Townsend Analytics, Ltd.

SanDisk Corporation

When an expansion-of-range-and-volume move is so large that a measured move represents an unreasonable expectation for an extension, I use 150% Fibonacci expansions to project price. What defines reasonable is subjective, but by watching many examples of the expansion-of-range-and-volume-news-event set-ups play out, traders should become comfortable assessing when it is unlikely for the follow-through move to double the initial gain. The SanDisk Corporation (SNDK) example in Figure 6.6 is one of the more obvious examples I encountered in 2012.

SNDK is frequently the subject of takeover chatter, and the moves that follow the news are often quite volatile. In Figure 6.6, the **flyonthewall.com** alert is followed by a $0.93-per-share expansion-of-range-and-volume move that took the stock from the central pivot, through R1, and continued moving higher. The magnitude of the move prompted me to use a 1.50 Fibonacci expansion as the target, rather than a measured move or an R2 pivot extension. The resulting trade triggered a long entry at $36.10, with an exit at the $36.52 Fibonacci extension.

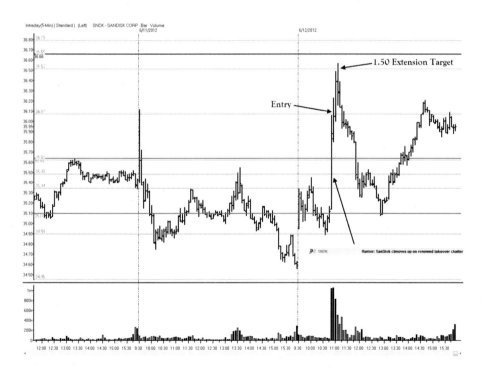

FIGURE 6.6 – SANDISK CORPORATION
RealTick by Townsend Analytics, Ltd.

Fusion-IO Inc

Fusion-IO Inc (FIO) provides another example (Figure 6.7) of an expansion-of-range-and-volume move that is more suitable for a Fibonacci-expansion target than for a measured move or pivot-extension projection. The stock made a two-pivot move immediately after renewed takeover chatter started circulating. A measured-move extension would require the stock to travel nearly another dollar per share, without a significant retracement, while the 1.50 Fibonacci extension represented $0.45 per share, a much more reasonable move based on the stock's normal five-minute travel range. Once FIO reached the $33.70 target it quickly reversed, triggering an exit just below the target.

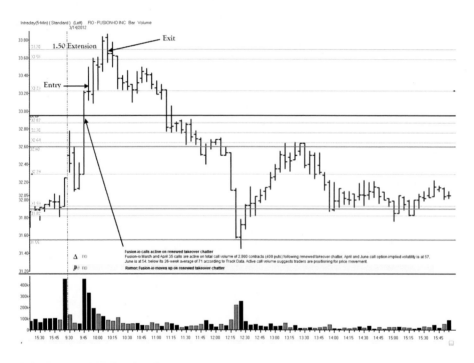

FIGURE 6.7 – FUSION-IO INC
RealTick by Townsend Analytics, Ltd.

Playing Both Sides of the News

An intraday strategy that finds opportunity in directional momentum can usually find additional opportunity when the euphoria of a sudden big move wears off. A strong thrust on circulating takeover chatter almost always reverses course for at least a few bars. Often times, the reversal can last for hours, creating a short entry opportunity with high profit potential.

As with the discretionary long-side entry on the initial chatter, the reversal entry requires a very keen awareness of everything that is contributing to price action. The key to identifying positions with potential is to look for the telltale signs of a big picture reversal. Decreasing volume and selling activity on the time of sales screen will provide strong indications that a push higher is likely to retrace. Price bars that stall out and close inside the range of the previous bar also suggest that the push may be over.

When reversal behaviours overlap, there is a strong case to be made for experienced traders to consider the short entry. If I am presented with this opportunity, the first thing I do is look for a suitable target and stop. If the profit-to-loss ratio on the trade is acceptable, I will take a position and look for an opportunity to capitalise on the reversal of fortune as the takeover chatter excitement gives way to profit-taking and ultimately panic-selling.

Wellcare Health Plans Inc

Wellcare Health Plans Inc (WCG) made an expansion-of-range-and-volume move after newswires reported takeover chatter. But the $1.82 initial thrust was an extension that had traders backing away to give the stock some room to breathe. Contracting volatility and decreasing volume left the WCG just below R1 pivot support with a logical short-sale-reversal entry at $54.45, just below the low of the narrowest range bar in the volatility contraction. The logical profit target for the WCG reversal entry was at natural support and resistance which was present at two levels – $54.20 and $54.10. This channel represented the final consolidation in the previous session's trading, and WCG dropped precisely to the lower band of that channel before reversing and trending higher for the balance of the session.

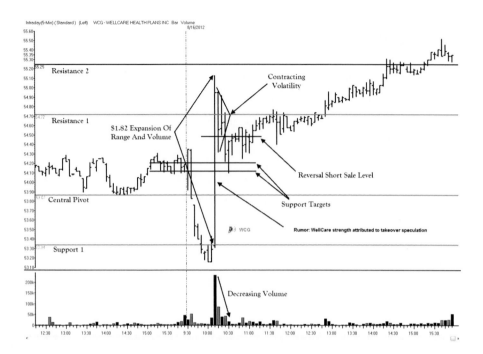

FIGURE 6.8 – WELLCARE HEALTH PLANS INC
RealTick by Townsend Analytics, Ltd.

Summary

Intraday set-ups after news events develop very quickly and are definitely best left to very experienced traders. Because of intraday noise and the instability of chart patterns in very short time compressions, the trader who wishes to find opportunity intraday needs to develop flexible thinking and look for set-ups that represent the spirit of important daily chart patterns, like the expansion-of-range-and-volume set-up considered here. When executed by someone who is comfortable gauging price action in fast markets, these quick scalps can definitely add to the bottom line. They can also develop into session-long positions and generate significant gains. Traders who are uncomfortable dealing with the pace of the set-up should avoid it until they have more experience in the time frame.

CHAPTER 7.
The Sinker 52-Week-High Reversal

T HE EXPANSION-OF-RANGE-AND-VOLUME trade is a cornerstone of my business. As with the other strategies covered in this book, I capitalise on variations of the expansion-of-range-and-volume set-up with the 52-week-high reversal pattern. When it comes on the heels of a shallow pullback or range consolidation, it is a reliable volatility play that frequently hands over substantial profits. Applied properly, it is stable, reliable, and easy to plan and execute.

When the market gets overextended, this range expansion set-up at new highs can generate strong reversals that are frustrating and can quickly yield a loss rather than a profit. While some traders may be tempted to simply adopt a rule stating that expansions at new highs are not to be traded, I evaluate the situation differently. If a pattern failure is predictable, it is not a problem; it is an opportunity. I call this particular opportunity a *sinker*, and when it forms on the daily chart, the intraday profit potential is substantial.

The tendency for markets to get overextended is a given. Since the 1990s, we have seen the market swing wildly to extreme extensions only to eventually reverse course and revert to a mean that could have been predicted with a simple trend line. A 'normal' market with smooth trends followed by long periods of consolidation and orderly pullbacks is now more the aberration than the norm. Instead, violent moves higher and lower dominate the price action. Market tops happen at technical levels that trigger calamitous moves lower, undoing months of constructive price action in just a few weeks. This is a phenomenon that has created much confusion among members of the buy-and-hold crowd. The uncertainty that accompanies confusion can create some great opportunities when these traditional investors and some of their trader counterparts jump in and out of the broader market, pushing the indices into heavy bouts of profit-taking.

The same holds true for individual equities. When a stock makes a sharp move higher without taking time to consolidate or pull back in an orderly fashion, and then hits a key technical inflection level, the stage is set for heavy profit-taking. The presence of a 52-week high is the technical level that I am most interested in when evaluating a potential sinker candidate.

A violent expansion move that ends with a one-year high tends to pull many inexperienced traders into the market as they are evaluating the quality of the stock only by its ability to make new highs. Everyone who has read a popular investing publication is familiar with the concept of buying strength, so the notion of buying new highs is likely to be an investor mainstay for some time. The problem is that there are many traders who have seen reactions to new highs on parabolic price extensions in the past, and they are looking to take the other side of any buyer's trade. They will look for the first sign of weakness as a stock fails to follow through, and exit a long position or establish a short when it appears that there is trouble brewing. Their selling activity begets more selling. Progressively more people who were fortunate enough to buy low pile on to sell high. As the selling intensifies, the unlucky 52-week-high buyers will start covering their losses. In the course of this selling, there is substantial opportunity for short-side profit.

Remember, fear is always more powerful than greed.

When I see a stock making a parabolic climb that culminates in an expansion-of-range-and-volume move, I immediately drill down into the intraday price action to see what happened as the stock reached new highs. I look for a significant expansion range. Generally, I want to see a move at least 50% greater than the range on a typical day in the climb. I also want to see that the closing activity did not include large block transactions at the asking price. When all this is in place, I prepare myself for the reversal entry.

The day after the expansion bar I look for early signs of last-minute buying. Usually this happens immediately after the market open as retail traders who learned of the 52-week high after the closing bell use market orders to buy the open. If these orders are not followed by additional strength, I look to short the stock just below the prior session high and target a move back into the travel range.

The rules for the set-up are in Figure 7.1 and are as follows:

1. A stock makes a swing low and then makes a very strong trending move without pausing for an orderly pull back or consolidation.

2. Price moves higher in an expansion of range and volume that culminates with a 52-week high.

3. On the trigger day, traders buy the stock in early trading, pushing price just above the expansion-day high where it meets with selling pressure. Short the stock as it moves lower through the expansion-of-range-and-volume closing price. The initial target is a 50% retracement of the expansion-day bar. The stop is .10–.30 above the expansion-day high.

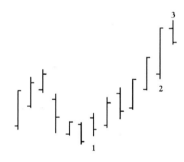

FIGURE 7.1
RealTick by Townsend Analytics, Ltd.

The Role of the Broader Markets

The sinker variation of the expansion-of-range-and-volume set-up works very well when the broader averages are at or near 52-week highs, or are having difficulty penetrating overhead resistance, as the pattern sets up in an individual stock. If the sector to which an equity is correlated is having difficulty penetrating resistance and moving higher, I take a closer look at the stock. This will shed some light on the probability of a profitable outcome.

Remember that the pattern is only valid after a persistent, non-consolidating trend with few pullbacks. This means that it will not occur regularly if the markets are trading in an orderly fashion. But when a runaway market rules the day, as it did in 2007, or when markets are attempting to move higher through significant overhead resistance as they were in 2011, the opportunities are relatively easy to find.

Notice in Figure 7.2 that the Dow Jones Industrials made a near-parabolic 1,800 point move higher in October of 2011 (1). When the index was unable to break higher (1–4), price action began a wide-volatility range. This indicated that future price action could include violent swings. Ultimately, that proved to be the case, as the markets exhibited extreme volatility (both good and bad) over the next 12 months of trading.

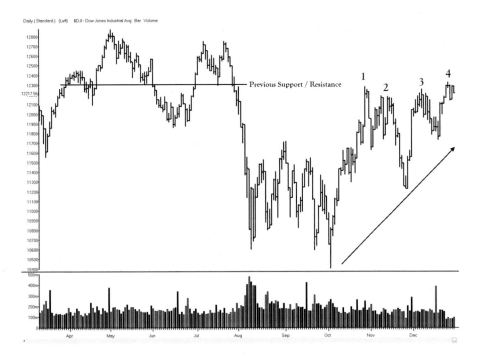

Daily (Standard) (Left) $DJI-Dow Jones Industrial Avg Bar Volume

Previous Support / Resistance

FIGURE 7.2 – DOW JONES INDUSTRIAL AVERAGE
RealTick by Townsend Analytics, Ltd.

The important thing to note in Figure 7.2 is what was happening at the time the chart was unfolding. I did not know whether the industrial stocks would ultimately move higher or lower, but I did know that a topping formation was occurring and that this would lead traders and investors who bought stocks to be very cautious about holding them if a reversal unfolded.

When this scenario plays out, I start looking for the sinker set-up on the daily charts. Finding stocks that are breaking to new highs on expanded volume with no consolidation or pullback is really just a matter of quickly flipping through charts and finding candidates. In the absence of the other expansion-of-range-and-volume criteria, it is a fast process.

Netsuite Inc

Netsuite Inc (N) is a stock that has all the right ingredients when it comes to trading intraday. The volume is good, but not heavy, making smoother moves than very thinly traded or heavily traded securities. When the stock sets up any of my pattern entries, it generally has good follow-through. As a member of the information technology group, its correlation to the sector and broader indices is frequently strong enough to create predictable moves that make sense when viewed together with what is happening in the markets.

These are all factors that I consider when making my selections for the stocks I trade every day, and are they particularly important with a pattern like sinker. It is very important that traders are intimately acquainted with the personality of the securities being traded. Some stocks will be easier to follow than others. There are many stocks that I will ignore no matter how good a set-up looks because these stocks have taught me some painful lessons.

When N generated a sinker set-up, I knew that a downdraft would present a reliable profit opportunity for the stock. As shown in Figure 7.3, N did not disappoint.

FIGURE 7.3 – NETSUITE INC (I)
RealTick by Townsend Analytics, Ltd.

1. N makes a persistent trending move higher.

2. An expansion-of-range-and-volume outside day extends the recent move without an orderly pullback or consolidation, and N is trading at a 52-week high. Notice that, although volume on the expansion day was significant, it was not as strong as I would have liked to see according to the criteria added in Chapter 3. This was actually preferable for the sinker set-up, as heavy volume indicated a higher probability of follow-through. The trade would also have been viable if the stock had closed slightly off its highs as opposed to closing in the very top of the range.

3. N attempted to break higher in early trading, reversed through the entry level and triggered a short position. The gain on the trade was $0.60 per share.

Figure 7.4 illustrates the handling of the trade intraday and should clarify any questions about what constitutes an attempted breakout.

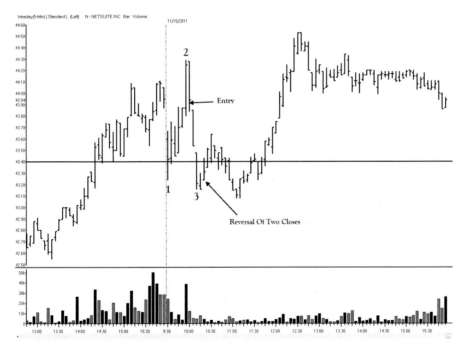

FIGURE 7.4 – NETSUITE INC (II)
RealTick by Townsend Analytics, Ltd.

1. N opened lower on the session, and traded at the initial profit target before turning higher. The price activity at the support/resistance line has me confident that the target is a good place to exit a short position if it triggers later in the session.

2. A steady climb higher during the first 30 minutes of trading has N testing new 52-week highs. The stock makes an intraday reversal move that I call a kings and queens reversal and travels lower, triggering the entry just below the prior session's close

3. The stock trades through the initial profit target and triggers an exit on a reversal of two closing prices.

Runaway markets are very easy to find, as price action that normally takes years to unfold occurs in progressively shorter amounts of time. Today, the proximity of a market to significant technical support and resistance dictates how economic, earnings and filing statements will be interpreted. If the market is making lows at previous support and the news is good, the indices will shoot higher. Oddly enough, they will do the same if the news is only mediocre. Once the low support range is cleared, every bit of data, so long as it is at least not as bad as expected, will push prices higher. Then when the market reaches overhead resistance, the opposite phenomenon will take hold. Suddenly, the news can never be quite good enough, and the market will rapidly deconstruct itself.

This was certainly the case in 2011. The market was constantly handed dire news. The economy showed signs of becoming deflationary, consumer sentiment was awful, and news from America's major corporations implied that the economic recovery was stalling out and that corporate earnings were in danger. Yet the news was not as bad as it could have been, and that served to propel the Dow Jones Industrials from a support low at 12,035 to a resistance high at 13,593 in just four months time (Figure 7.5). Once again, the price action in the major indices going into the end of 2011 indicated that there would be sinker set-ups to capitalise on as the year came to a close.

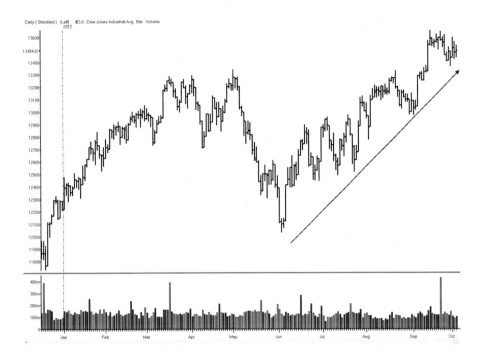

FIGURE 7.5 – DOW JONES INDUSTRIAL AVERAGE
RealTick by Townsend Analytics, Ltd.

Eli Lilly & Co.

Eli Lilly & Co. (LLY) followed the market's lead in 2011 by putting in a move higher that had the stock at 52-week highs with relatively little good news along the way. When the stock formed a daily reversal set-up in late December, all the pieces were in place for a quick profit (Figure 7.6).

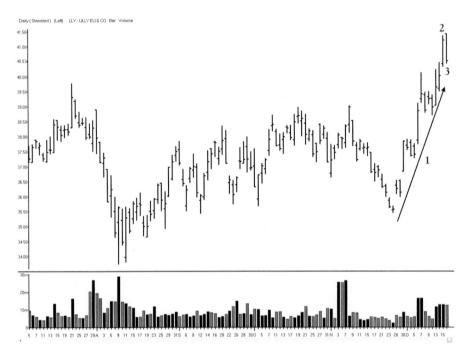

FIGURE 7.6 – ELI LILLY & CO. (I)
RealTick by Townsend Analytics, Ltd.

1. LLY made a strong trending move higher, adding 18% to its share price in just under a month. The stock paused and made a minor swing low, but did not significantly retrace any of the major move to highs.

2. A 52-week high and an expansion of range and volume set up the stock for a sinker reversal.

3. On the trigger day, the stock tried to push higher, but made a perfect sinker reversal instead.

Once again, the intraday chart shows how the set-up played out in the five-minute time compression.

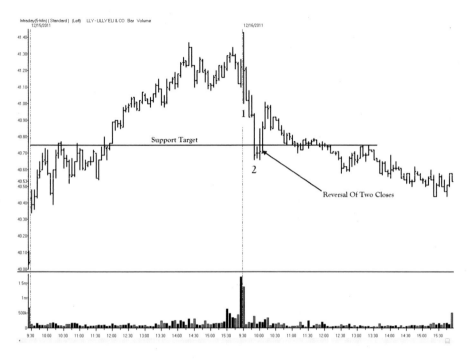

FIGURE 7.7 – ELI LILLY & CO. (II)
RealTick by Townsend Analytics, Ltd.

1. LLY opened, traded higher, and reversed and triggered a short position. Volume increased as the stock passed through the previous session's high, indicating that overnight holders of the stock were attempting to take the money and run.

2. LLY made a move lower for a slight extension of the profit target, yielding $0.43 per share after a reversal-of-two-closes exit.

Centene Corp

Although the news for the health care sector indicated that stocks in the group would head lower, some of the big names in the group were firmly higher in late 2011. Centene Corp (CNC) was one of the beneficiaries of the momentum and was on course for stellar performance. When what started out as a retracement turned into a gap-and-go move instead, a sinker set-up was the most likely outcome (Figure 7.8).

FIGURE 7.8 – CENTENE CORP (I)
RealTick by Townsend Analytics, Ltd.

1. A gap higher moves CNC out of a retracement to congestion support, and the stock trades just below recent resistance.

2. Three days of constructive price action culminate with an expansion-of-range move to 52-week highs. Volume decreases on each progressively higher day, indicating a strong probability of a move lower.

3. The stock made a minor move higher, then reversed and retraced 50% of the set-up day's price bar.

The intraday examples should make this atypical strategy easier to understand. In the case of Centene Corp, the example of the 50% support retracement target develops perfectly (Figure 7.9).

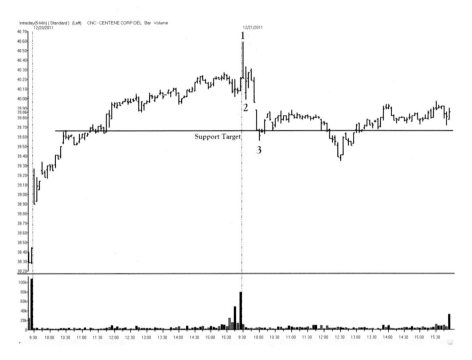

FIGURE 7.9 – CENTENE CORP (II)
RealTick by Townsend Analytics, Ltd.

1. The stock opened flat and moved rapidly higher, making another new 52-week high on light opening volume. This was a sign that the pros were removing themselves from the order flow and retail buyers were filled near the market open.

2. A fast reversal lower triggered the short entry.

3. The stock moved $0.43 per share to the initial profit target.

Plains All American Pipeline LP

Plains All American Pipeline LP (PAA) trades at the low end of average daily volume for an energy stock, but this serves to push the stock very rapidly once it gains momentum. When PAA made a big move in December 2011, the expansion of range that led to a 52-week high was on unimpressive volume, even for PAA. This told me that the odds of a sinker reversal day were relatively high for the next session (Figure 7.10).

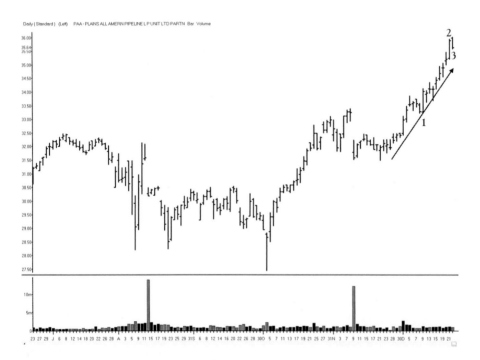

FIGURE 7.10 – PLAINS ALL AMERICAN PIPELINE LP (I)
RealTick by Townsend Analytics, Ltd.

1. PAA moved higher throughout December. The stock never paused to consolidate or retrace any of its gains.

2. An expansion-of-range move higher put the stock in 52-week-high territory and set up a sinker pattern entry for the following session.

3. The stock traded higher and reversed, yielding $0.43 per share over the course of the session.

While the sinker set-up frequently triggers right around the open, this is not a requirement for the trade. In the case of Plains All American Pipeline LP, there was a push to yet another 52-week high soon after the opening bell. This happened on relatively moderately high volume and was followed by an equally high volume sell-off. In this case, the stock took 15 minutes to trigger an entry, and illustrates the need to stay vigilant around the open (Figure 7.11).

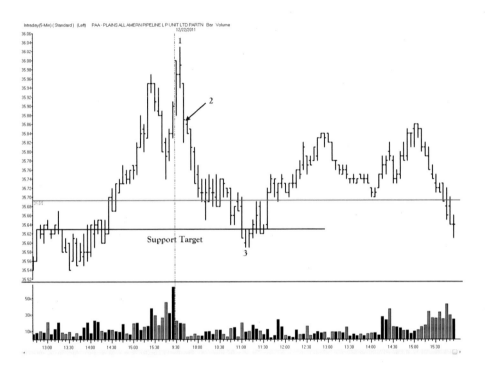

FIGURE 7.11 – PLAINS ALL AMERICAN PIPELINE LP (II)
RealTick by Townsend Analytics, Ltd.

1. PAA opened and traded to a new 52-week high on high volume.

2. The stock triggered an entry fifteen minutes into the trading day.

3. PAA trended lower and reached the intraday support target.

Target Corp

In an imperfect world, I think it is important to point out the efficacy of less-than-perfect set-ups. In Figure 7.12, Target Corp (TGT) provides an example, as traders needed to find the set-up on the heels of a lengthy 2012 congestion range.

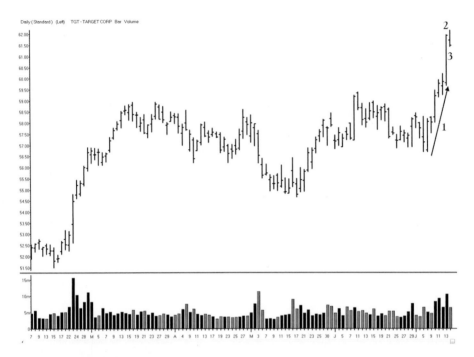

FIGURE 7.12 – TARGET CORP (I)
RealTick by Townsend Analytics, Ltd.

1. TGT spends much of 2011 in a volatile, choppy, sideways congestion range. Then, in July, the stock makes a rapid expansion move.

2. TGT makes a 52-week high. The expansion-of-range-and-volume move qualifies as a sinker set-up, and my plan is to take a short position on a breakdown through the set-up day closing price.

3. On the reversal day, the stock fails to follow through to the target, but still manages to book a profit for the trade.

4. The trigger day was also less than perfect and required some discipline. While it is actually a relatively simple matter to find the picture-perfect set-ups, the

less-than-perfect trade is illustrative of the thought process a trader needs to follow to stay on the right side of opportunity (Figure 7.13).

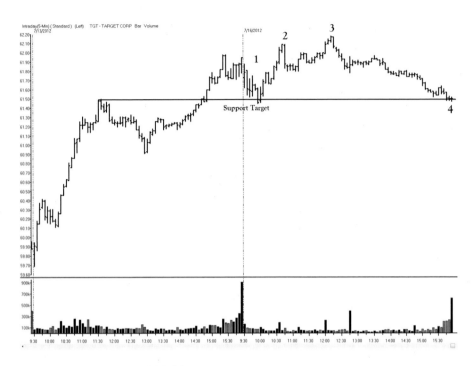

FIGURE 7.13 – TARGET CORP (II)
RealTick by Townsend Analytics, Ltd.

1. The stock opened slightly lower and proceeded to trade below the prior session's closing range for an hour.

2. Low volume buying managed to push TGT to another 52-week high, and the reversal move triggered a short-sale entry. The result of the trade was a loss of $0.10 per share, as TGT traded back up through the previous close.

3. TGT qualified another entry, trading above the previous close to yet another 52-week high.

4. Another entry trigger, and TGT started a low-volume move that would take the stock slowly lower for several hours.

5. The trade is closed at the end of the session for a net gain of $0.26 per share.

Summary

There are special circumstances required for the sinker trade to be included in my trading plan, but when the criteria are met, this is a very profitable set-up. The high probability of follow-through on the trigger day makes this a favourite for me and my subscribers.

The nature of the set-up dictates that the rules are a little looser than most newer traders prefer. But once the tenets of the expansion-of-range-and-volume paradigm are clearly understood, this derivative strategy should make perfect sense. That it sometimes occurs under less-than-ideal pattern conditions is a by-product of the precursor for the set-up being essentially a pattern failure. With a little practice, I think most traders will see the value in searching for opportunities with this powerful reversal strategy.

CHAPTER 8.
Establishing Big-Picture Positions

I THINK THAT MOST technical patterns are best developed in a short time frame and then tested for robustness in progressively larger ones. This may seem counterintuitive as data in the shorter time frame is more difficult to work with than longer compressions are, but it has worked well for me.

There are more conditions that need to be considered in the tighter confines of intraday trading than in swing and position trading. Intraday data can be difficult to interpret because there are so many different ways to consolidate it. But in the end, all the different views make for some very solid models that wind up being very portable. Once a strategy has been refined and works well intraday, it should work well across multiple time frames as long as it relies on price and time and not intraday indicators for decision-making. This is the key to success in trading – find something that works and then do it consistently.

I would assert that there is no right way to think. How people see things is a matter of how they are wired. In my case, I like to observe things in the present. I do not like to look back at charts and try to reconstruct what happened. I develop theories by planning today and doing tomorrow. My longer-term methodologies extrapolate from my core ideas and perform equally well whether handling big picture trades or when operating in the intraday arena. This discipline is what I use for intermediate-term planning, and in the institutional advisory service that I provide through Trireme Capital Advisors, LLC.

When focusing on swing trading, there are a few changes that must to be made to the basic set-up in order for it to provide a sustainable profit strategy. There is an additional screening tool used by many swing traders that helps make the trades more reliable. It is a shift to the shorter time frame to spot stop levels. To be a successful day, swing or position trader, traders need to shift time frames often when doing research. The market does not choose to work according to your preferences. Too many people fail in this business because they restrict themselves to one view of the markets based on their time bias. The market is made up of millions upon millions of participants. Market participants all see things a little differently, so traders need to take as many of these beliefs into account when planning trades. This dramatically increases your prospects of success.

The criteria for a good expansion-of-range-and-volume set-up are the same in the longer time compressions as they are for the daily set-up. In the case of the swing or position trade, the only difference is that we are looking for the set-ups on weekly charts, establishing stops on weekly and daily charts, and finding targets on weekly and monthly charts. The fact that I do not rely on indicators to develop an entry candidate works in my favour when shifting time frames. Indicators are generally not predictable across compressions, and often the effort to adjust their settings to accommodate the shift invalidates the basic assumptions that define their use. Relying on price, volume and time puts a focus on the core components that affect market behaviour, allowing for observation and planning based on the purest form of market data.

In this chapter, I again demonstrate the efficacy of my process by using some real-life trading examples. As I proceed, remember that swing and day trading are different animals and require a very different perception of risk and reward. While an intraday trader may look at a potential gain of .50 per share and deem it a fantastic return, any swing trader would most likely call that number completely unacceptable. This, of course, stems from the fact that day traders tie up their trading capital for minutes and use leverage of as much as 4:1, while swing traders tie up their money for days to months at a time and use leverage of 2:1. The longer holding period and larger capital requirements necessitate trades with wide targets and, consequently, wide stops.

Amerigroup Corp

Figure 8.1 shows the utility of the set-up in identifying potential swing and position trades. Amerigroup Corp (AGP) made a persistent trending move higher on the weekly chart (1) and then formed a downward sloping consolidation range (2). So far everything looked just as it does when the ideal pattern set-up appears in the daily time frame. AGP broke lower on an expansion-of-range-and-volume set-up (3) and closed in the bottom 25% of its weekly range. Previous support and resistance was evident in 2010, when a strong clustering of highs around $56.34 developed a zone that acted as a strong profit target for the trade being considered.

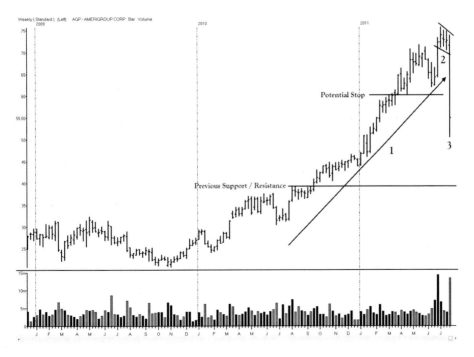

FIGURE 8.1 – AMERIGROUP CORP (I)
RealTick by Townsend Analytics, Ltd.

Looking for a stop in the weekly time frame can be tricky. In the case of AGP, the first place to look was at a move back into the support and resistance range that developed during the trend move (1) in Figure 8.1. But examining the daily chart (Figure 8.2) revealed that a more conservative and equally valid stop was available at $56.34. The daily move would require the reversal of a very large amount of price action, including a large-volume gap that moved price lower by $6.00 per share. This area accounted for some of the gap region, but did not require as significant a retracement move before triggering an exit. The reward-to-risk ratio on the set-up was 1.85:1, within the acceptable range for a big-picture position.

The weekly chart of the expansion-of-range-and-volume set-up does not show this large gap move.

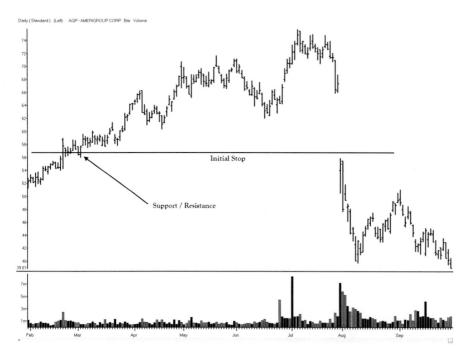

FIGURE 8.2 – AMERIGROUP CORP (II)
RealTick by Townsend Analytics, Ltd.

As seen in Figure 8.3, AGP triggered an entry and made a $9.00 move in favour of the set-up. A profit-protecting-loss was placed just above recent resistance on the weekly chart. A previous test of this area had taken price nearly all the way to the entry trigger, and a second violation could retrace much of the move. Volume was also on the increase again, with volume on up days being greater than volume on down days. This was also a sign of a potential reversal in the making.

After a nine-week move, AGP hit the target price, right on top of multiple time frame support and resistance (Figure 8.4). The net profit for the trade was $11.00 per share.

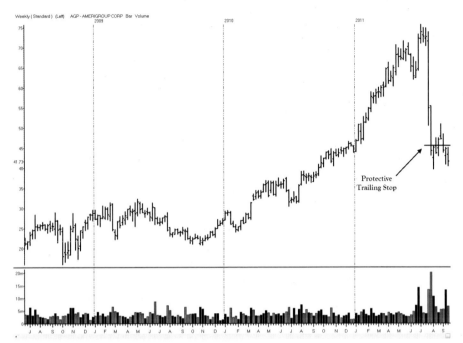

FIGURE 8.3 – AMERIGROUP CORP (III)
RealTick by Townsend Analytics, Ltd.

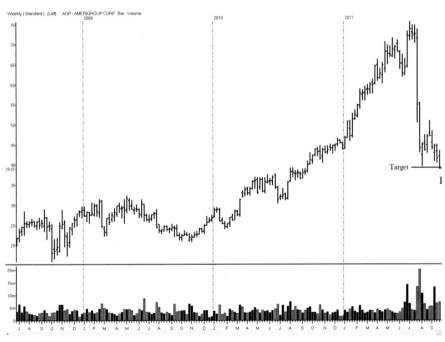

FIGURE 8.4 – AMERIGROUP CORP (IV)
RealTick by Townsend Analytics, Ltd.

BMC Software Inc.

Figure 8.5 shows that BMC Software Inc. (BMC) spent much of 2010 in a trending move higher (1). As BMC moved higher, there were multiple weeks in which it traded on substantial range and volume, but the stock never offered a solid expansion-of-range-and-volume set-up. It definitely seemed as though the second half of 2010 was characterised by missed opportunity as the stock continued to gain momentum. Then, after a 2010 year-end consolidation, 2011 began with a widening range and another push higher with no discernible pattern entries. By May and June of 2011, the stock attempted to break the high of a consolidation range at $56.00 per share (2). In late July, BMC rolled over, began moving lower and made an expansion-of-range-and-volume move through the bottom of the consolidation that left BMC at $43.22 a share.

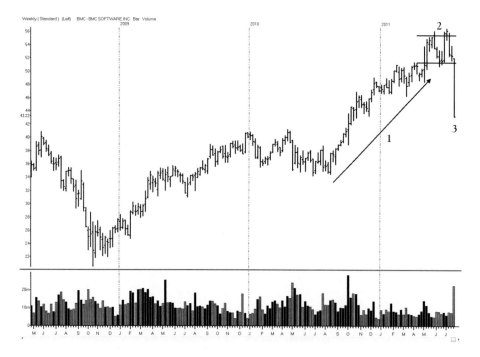

FIGURE 8.5 – BMC SOFTWARE INC. (I)
RealTick by Townsend Analytics, Ltd.

A target for an extension of the expansion-of-range-and-volume move was evident on the weekly chart, where multiple confluent areas of support and resistance at $38.97 were obvious as far back as 2008 (Figure 8.6). Coupled with a short-sale entry price at $43.01, and a stop loss based on late 2010 $45.13 overhead resistance, the trade set-up yielded a 1.91:1 reward-to-risk ratio, and became a planned set-up for my *Around The Horn Swing Trading Plan* for 1 August 2011 as seen on page 100. BMC triggered an entry and achieved the profit target over the course of two weeks (Figure 8.7).

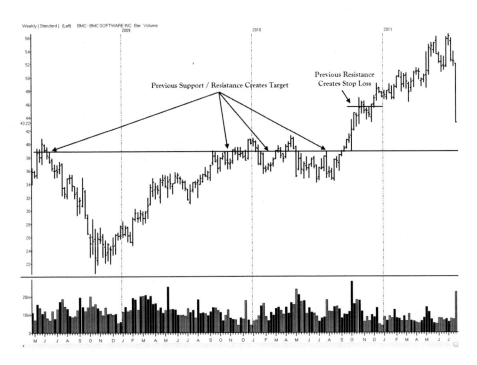

FIGURE 8.6 – BMC SOFTWARE INC. (II)
RealTick by Townsend Analytics, Ltd.

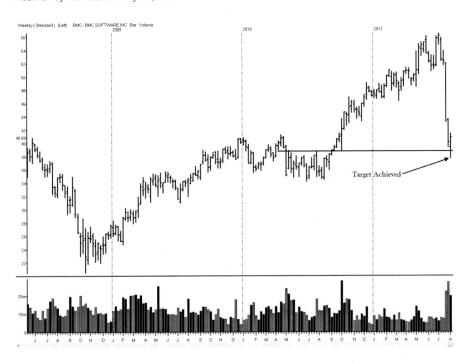

FIGURE 8.7 – BMC SOFTWARE INC. (III)
RealTick by Townsend Analytics, Ltd.

Around The Horn Swing Plan
Monday, August 01, 2011

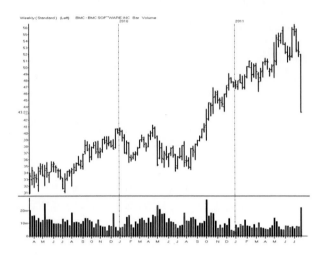

Symbol	BMC	
Description	BMC SOFTWARE INC	
Pattern	XRV	
Position	Short	
Entry	43.01	
Stop	45.13	GICS
Initial Target	38.97	Software
Ratio	1.91	Information Technology
50% To Target	40.99	Systems Software

BMC PLAN

Harsco Corporation

Harsco Corporation (HSC) made many expansion-of-range-and-volume moves from 2009–11. Almost all of these were profitable, as HSC showed a propensity for follow-through. When the stock had another textbook set-up in July 2011, I was eager to take advantage of the opportunity for a fast short-sale move.

In Figure 8.8, HSC exhibits all of the characteristics of a good trade in the making. The weekly time frame shows clear overhead resistance that has propelled the stock lower each time it has been tested since 2009. An initial target is easy to identify, as confluent support in 2009 and 2010 consistently stopped downward moves and reversed them higher. A stop loss was evident as well, as 2011 had started with a move higher from an area of resistance that had propelled the stock higher on five prior occasions. In the course of developing the expansion-of-range-and-volume set-up, HSC bounced off overhead resistance and the stop loss level twice. The second move lower from resistance (1) led to a shallow pullback (2) and a high volume sell-off. The expansion-of-range-and-volume bar developed on nearly triple-average volume, and left a planned entry at $26.33, a stop loss at $28.22, and a target at $21.43. The reward-to-risk ratio for the short-sale trade was 2.59:1, and the set-up was part of my plan for 1 August 2011.

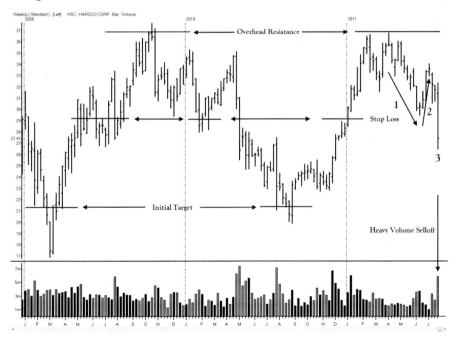

FIGURE 8.8 – HARSCO CORPORATION (I)
RealTick by Townsend Analytics, Ltd.

HSC made another expansion-of-range-and-volume move during the week that the trade triggered (Figure 8.9), and achieved the profit target the following week. When expansion-of-range-and-volume moves come on the heels of each other, it is normally a good idea to look for an opportunity to take a profit, as additional extensions, especially beyond a logical target, are unlikely. Traders looking for additional profitability in the direction of the original set-up can shift time compressions and look for opportunities for re-entry after a pullback on a daily chart with an objective at the initial profit target.

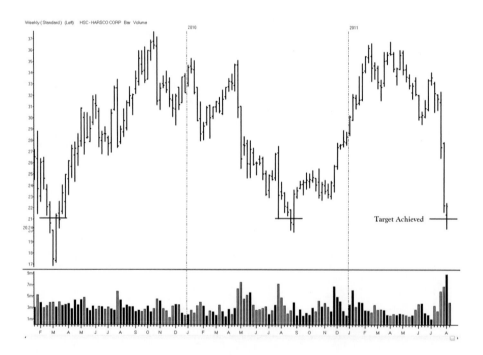

FIGURE 8.9 – HARSCO CORPORATION (II)
RealTick by Townsend Analytics, Ltd.

Sherwin Williams Co

When the weekly chart of Sherwin Williams Co (SHW) developed an expansion-of-range-and-volume set-up, the pattern seemed to offer a large potential for a significant gain. Figure 8.10 shows five measured moves the stock made from April 2010 to December 2011. Three of these moves were approximately $16.00, the other two were $11.18. The weekly chart also provided a clear stop loss for any long position in the stock at $85.69. A planned entry at $90.32, with a conservative target at $101.50, gave the trade a 2.41:1 reward-to-risk ratio, and the possibility of a profit extension made the ratio even better. The trade set-up (as seen on page 104) was sent to my subscribers for the week of 26 December 2011.

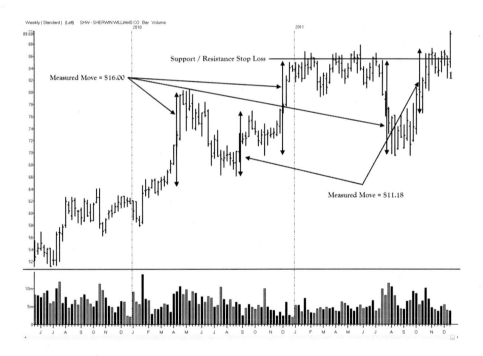

FIGURE 8.10 – SHERWIN WILLIAMS CO (I)
RealTick by Townsend Analytics, Ltd.

Around The Horn Swing Plan
Monday, December 26, 2011

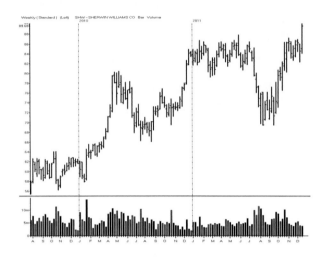

Symbol	SHW		
Description	SHERWIN WILLIAMS CO		
Pattern	XRV		
Position	Long		
Entry	90.32		
Stop	85.69	GICS	
Initial Target	101.50	Chemicals	
Ratio	2.41	Materials	
50% To Target	95.91	Specialty Chemicals	

SHW PLAN

Figure 8.11 shows the result of the SHW trade, and also illustrates clearly the benefit of trading in multiple time frames. SHW barely triggered the expansion-of-range-and-volume entry, and did very little by way of constructive price movement in the first week that the position was open. In the following weeks, however, SHW moved cleanly through both of the measured move projections, and never showed any signs of a starting a reversal. Carrying even a portion of the position with an eight-period SMA stop (discussed in *Beat the Street: A Trader's Guide to Consistently Profiting in the Markets*) resulted in an exit on a violation of the moving average at $116.41 for a $26.05 gain on the balance of the trade.

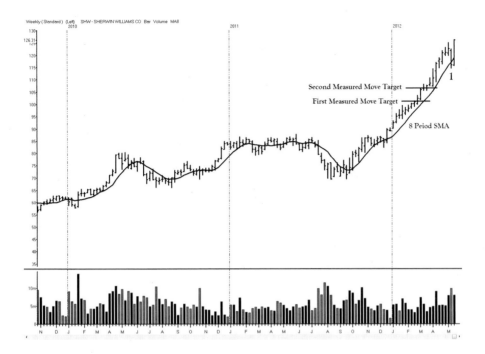

Weekly (Standard) (Left) SHW - SHERWIN WILLIAMS CO Bar Volume MA8

Second Measured Move Target

First Measured Move Target

8 Peiod SMA

FIGURE 8.11 – SHERWIN WILLIAMS CO (II)
RealTick by Townsend Analytics, Ltd.

Summary

Applying the expansion-of-range-and-volume set-up to the swing or position trading time frame further demonstrates the flexibility of this set-up. Using a longer time frame makes it possible for money managers and traders who do not want to sit in front of the screen all day, every day, to capitalise on one of the best trading strategies I have ever found. While some of the parameters need to change to accommodate the goals of a longer time frame, the basic principles are the same.

CHAPTER 9.
The Vertically Integrated Trader

THE STRATEGIES I HAVE discussed in this book represent a powerful trading paradigm that allows traders to capitalise on a proven phenomenon in multiple time frames with multiple objectives. The expansion set-ups that I have discussed use market volatility as a means of spotting and filtering opportunity. They are capable of producing profits for day traders, scalpers and swing traders. But the real promise awaits those who learn to apply the concepts to multiple time frames as part of a vertical trading business.

We are often told that to succeed as traders we need to make a choice. We can be intraday traders, scalpers, swing traders or position traders; but we cannot possibly be expected to do several of these things well. The truth, however, is that a trader is a trader. A view of the market that encompasses all possible holding periods opens a trading business up to many possible income streams.

Trading today is very different to what it was in the late 1990s. The ability to have an account working for you even when the markets are not presenting many opportunities in a particular time frame is critical to longer-term success. For example, summertime trading has been particularly slow in the intraday time compressions for several years now. But expansion positions held over the summer have generated large profits. It used to be that when trading slowed down, I would just take time off and wait for volume to return. But as the quiet periods have become protracted, the reality of sitting on the sidelines has become less and less appealing.

My swing-trading friends have experienced a similar situation. They complain about periods that exhibit extreme volatility and cause overnight positions to gap into resting stops. The volatility that works to create profits intraday creates losses in the longer compression. I see this in the many reversals that occur after price reaches a logical support or resistance target intraday. Look back at the examples presented in earlier chapters and note how often the target price becomes the ultimate high or low for a stock, and how effective the intraday trades are in picking up fast profits when markets seem to be in a volatility expansion that would be counterproductive for swing trades.

Now look back at the examples of trades that were presented in the bigger picture compressions. They tended to occur when the intraday set-ups were not particularly prevalent. The multiple-week expansion set-up almost always occurs at times that are not likely to have daily price action creating opportunities for intraday trades. Turn to the appendix and look at the large number of expansion-of-range-and-volume set-ups that occurred in January 2010 and consider that this period contained almost no set-ups in the weekly compression. Learn to get in front of opportunity without regard to time frame. Learn to manage risk and expectancy correctly and you can easily make the shift from being a day trader, swing trader, scalper or position trader to being *a trader*.

The important thing to remember is that trading is a business that requires extreme discipline. Once a particular methodology has been mastered, the best traders will recognise that the effort that was spent in the process can reap many rewards and is transferable to many situations. To say that one is a day trader, swing trader or position trader, and is unwilling to consider working in any other modality is illogical. It may not be comfortable to attempt the shift in thinking that is required, but it makes for a better trader in every case. Trying to think outside the box is what gets people thinking and creative in the first place. New ideas create new opportunities and ultimately force a trader to constantly reassess and refine a methodology. It is this process that keeps trading interesting and lucrative.

The goal of this book is to foster a flexible thought process for my readers. I have sought here to demonstrate to aspiring traders and professionals alike that there is opportunity to be found in volatility and that the markets will always provide a road map for success if traders are willing to take the time to consider it. When the market is telling traders to trade longer term, traders can only be successful if they listen. When the market says to focus on the micro-environment, traders need to shift to an intraday approach or risk suffering volatility-based losses. And when the market tells traders that volatility will prevent them from profiting in any time compression, traders need to stay out and find some other way to occupy their time.

At the very least, I hope that this book has started you thinking about a different way to approach the business of trading. I believe that integrating the volatility-based paradigm into any approach to the markets will provide tremendous benefits. Ultimately, the price action traders rely on to earn a living needs to be understood as a cyclical creature. The approach presented here allows traders to draw maximum benefit from each phase of the cycle by exposing them to as many expansion phases as possible.

APPENDIX A.
Tricks of the Trade

T HE REAL PROMISE of the trading strategies discussed in this book awaits those who learn to apply the set-ups to multiple time frames as part of a vertical trading business.

I have emphasised the role of careful planning in making a trader successful. Long-time subscribers to my intraday trading plan know that I practise what I preach. The plan I publish every night is the same one that I trade myself, and it provides a level of detail about each position that catches new traders off guard. I get questions asking why so many variables are included, why I do not use more discretion, and why I am not more generous in computing the results for each trade when I report them to members of the service. The answers to these questions should be obvious by this time, but I will reiterate my points on methodology here just to reinforce what I think are some important concepts.

Parts of a Solid Plan

The variables that are included for each position cover the spectrum of obvious to obscure. Entry price, stop loss and initial profit target are examples of the former and should require no further explanation. Pivot lines represent potential inflection points and can be computed for any time frame in which a chart can be viewed. Having them in my trading plan tells me where price is likely to pause. They are a map of potential inflection points and help me to figure out what is going on during the trading session. As I show in this appendix, I use pivots as a way to gauge the viability of early entries and potential profit extensions. Whenever trading becomes even the least bit discretionary, they factor heavily into my decision-making.

Fifty-percent-to-the-target represents the level at which price has moved half the distance from the extreme of the set-up bar to the expected level of support or resistance, which is the probable reversal area for intraday price. Fifty percent is of course an important Fibonacci number and is a mathematical operator that many traders watch. Experience has taught me that a price move to the 50%-to-target level is the best point at which to start implementing trailing stops, with the first being at break-even.

The sector to which a stock's trading is most correlated in recent weeks helps me to make decisions about whether to enter early at a pivot or support and resistance level, or whether to attempt to trail stops after a stock hits its profit target. For example, if I am in a short position that is correlated to the energy sector and my profit objective is met, it is decision time. Whether or not I will give the position some room to move will depend in large part on what the underlying sector is doing. If it is moving lower and has been leading the stock during the session, I will let profits run. If it has been leading the stock throughout the session and is itself at a pivot inflection or other support level and reversing, I will take my profits and move on. If the stock and sector have been negatively correlated during the session, I will fade the sector action. And if the correlation is no longer valid I will ignore the sector data.

As to the role of discretion in my trading, I have many set-ups that allow for intraday decision-making. But the *Around The Horn Trading Plan* is intended to be my core strategy, and the trades in it are well developed and can be implemented automatically. They are the best teaching tool for aspiring intraday traders. The information is unambiguous and traders can get a feel for whether they are trading the way a professional trader would. This is also why the results are reported in the most conservative manner. The rules provided for the service are followed exactly in the daily reports, and traders who are trying to learn what the methodology is all about can do so without the frustration of having a teacher who injects subjective decisions where an objective procedure is expected.

I am presenting in this appendix all of the intraday expansion-of-range trades that were triggered in January 2012 from the *Around The Horn Trading Plan*. Nothing is skipped, and the actual narrative from my *Tricks Of The Trade* book is included for each trigger. I should note that January is always very profitable for the expansion-of-range-and-volume set-up, as good volatility is usually high, and stocks are on the move early in the year. January accounted for 17 triggered expansion trades on the service. The strategy generated $3.76 per share in profits. For the eight months of trading that have been completed as of the writing of this book, the strategy generated $11.45 per share.

My log for my wife's and my trading follows.

Around The Horn Plan
Friday, January 06, 2012

Symbol	AGP	Sector Symbol	$HCX.X
Description	AMERIGROUP CORP		
Pattern	XRV	Managed Health Care	

Position	Long		
Entry	62.75	Resistance 2	64.03
Stop	62.41	Resistance 1	63.27
Initial Target	63.25	Pivot	61.90
Ratio	1.47	Support 1	61.14
50% To Target	63.00	Support 2	59.77

AGP PLAN

FIGURE A.1 – AMERIGROUP CORP
RealTick by Townsend Analytics, Ltd.

It looks like the year is off to a good start, as volatility is pushing price rather than leading to choppy trading action. AGP benefited from the action in the broader indices this morning, with a high smooth move through an easy entry that provided follow-through after 45 minutes of consolidated trading. Price moved in our favour with no retracement, and traded right to the profit target and through the R1 resistance level. AGP consolidated above R1 briefly, then pushed higher and broke through R2.

AGP continued in a parabolic move to the upside and showed no sign of weakness until a four-dollar extension ended with a close in the bottom of an expansion bar. The next bar closed lower again and violated two closing prices, triggering an exit for a $3.25-per-share profit.

Around The Horn Plan
Friday, January 06, 2012

Symbol	HNT	Sector Symbol	$HCX.X
Description	HEALTH NET INC		
Pattern	XRV	Managed Health Care	

Position	Long	Resistance 2	32.32
Entry	31.68	Resistance 1	31.92
Stop	31.33	Pivot	31.17
Initial Target	32.16	Support 1	30.77
Ratio	1.37	Support 2	30.02
50% To Target	31.92		

INT PLAN

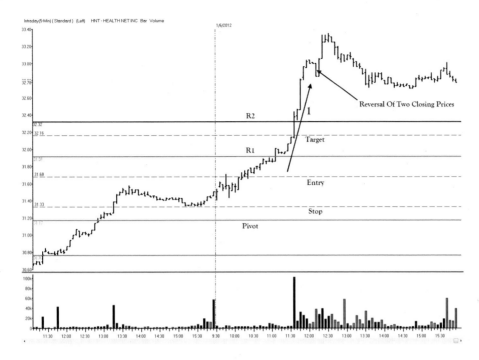

FIGURE A.2 – HEALTHNET INC
RealTick by Townsend Analytics, Ltd.

Healthnet (HNT) triggered and drifted lower this morning, staying just above the range high that consolidated yesterday's price going into the close of trading. Once the stock started moving, it did very well, as a slow and steady climb through R1, the initial target and R2 left little room for doubt as to the fact that HNT would put in an extension move. The push through R2 became parabolic (1), and just as I contemplated using an eight-period SMA to trail profits, the price action flattened out and had a reversal-of-two-closes violation. With the profit extension , the gain on the trade was $1.35 per share.

Around The Horn Plan
Monday, January 09, 2012

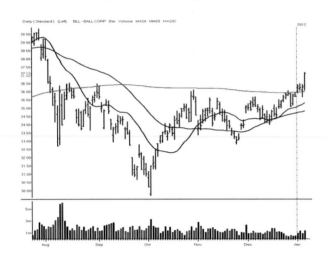

Symbol	BLL	Sector Symbol	$IXR
Description	BALL CORP		
Pattern	XRV	Metal & Glass Containers	

Position	Long	Resistance 2	37.89
Entry	37.28	Resistance 1	37.51
Stop	37.06	Pivot	36.79
Initial Target	37.55	Support 1	36.41
Ratio	1.23	Support 2	35.69
50% To Target	37.42		

BLL PLAN

FIGURE A.3 – BALL CORPORATION
RealTick by Townsend Analytics, Ltd.

Ball Corporation (BLL) opened flat on the session. The stock started climbing during the first five minutes of trading, and triggered an entry on moderate volume 20 minutes into the session. The stock never travelled .10 in our favour, but due to recent volatility in early trading, we have not been using the scratch stop in the first hour of the day. Even if we were using the rule, I would not apply it to this trade, as BLL has a $0.22 stop loss. With stocks with a stop this tight, applying the .10 rule is not useful, as two scratch stops, along with potential slippage, can result in a loss as great as the full stop out on the position.

BLL consolidated around the entry price and began moving lower at 11:00 ET. The stock hit the 37.06 stop and bounced. There was no opportunity for a second entry, and BLL traveled all the way to the central pivot, where it closed the day.

Around The Horn Plan
Thursday, January 12, 2012

Symbol	CBG		Sector Symbol	$IXF.X
Description	CBRE GROUP INC CL A			
Pattern	XRV		Real Estate Services	

Position	Long		Resistance 2	18.36
Entry	17.71		Resistance 1	17.96
Stop	17.47		Pivot	17.20
Initial Target	18.02		Support 1	16.80
Ratio	1.29		Support 2	16.04
50% To Target	17.87			

CBG PLAN

FIGURE A.4 – CBRE GROUP INC
RealTick by Townsend Analytics, Ltd.

CBRE Group Inc (CBG) seemed to be off to a good start this morning, as the stock made a wide range-opening move and triggered an entry right off the opening bell. Unfortunately, CBG only traveled in our favour for a few minutes before turning around and triggering our stop. The rest of the day offered no confirmation of the expansion-of-range-and-volume set-up, and the stock closed the day below the stop loss.

Around The Horn Plan
Thursday, January 12, 2012

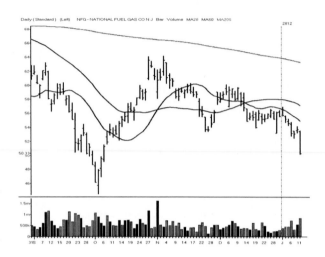

Symbol	NFG	Sector Symbol	$UTY.X
Description	NATIONAL FUEL GAS CO N J		
Pattern	XRV	Gas Utilities	

Position	Short	Resistance 2	54.73
Entry	50.11	Resistance 1	52.53
Stop	50.54	Pivot	51.37
Initial Target	49.54	Support 1	49.17
Ratio	1.33	Support 2	48.01
50% To Target	49.83		

NFG PLAN

FIGURE A.5 – NATIONAL FUEL GAS CO
RealTick by Townsend Analytics, Ltd.

National Fuel Gas Co (NFG) triggered a short-side entry on heavy opening volume. After traveling 50% of the distance to the initial profit target, the stock turned around and retraced the move, stopping out at the entry price. NFG traveled the required $0.08 above the entry, which served to reset the trading plan for the session. A second entry triggered 30 minutes into the session, and the resulting move extended through the profit target for an exit at the S1 pivot extension.

Around The Horn Plan
Thursday, January 19, 2012

Symbol	AVT	Sector Symbol	$XIT.X
Description	AVNET INC		
Pattern	XRV	Technology Distributors	

Position	Long	Resistance 2	35.84
Entry	34.20	Resistance 1	34.90
Stop	33.76	Pivot	33.16
Initial Target	34.79	Support 1	32.22
Ratio	1.34	Support 2	30.48
50% To Target	34.50		

AVT PLAN

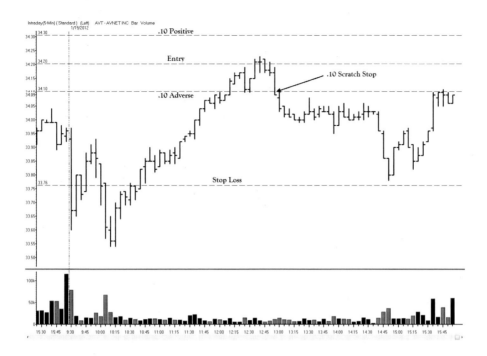

FIGURE A.6 – AVNET INC
RealTick by Townsend Analytics, Ltd.

Avnet Inc (AVT) did not show any early signs of follow-through this morning, as the stock opened flat then traded to the level of the stop loss. A slow climb higher over the course of the day had AVT at the trigger price by the noon hour. Because AVT had already been to the stop, and because the climb higher accounted for much of the stock's average daily range, we employed the .10 scratch stop rule for the position. The rule wound up saving us money, as AVT turned around and went .10 against us before traveling in our favour. The trade was exited for a loss of $0.10.

Around The Horn Plan
Thursday, January 19, 2012

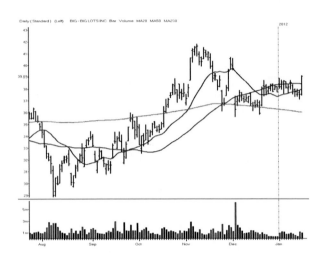

Symbol	BIG	Sector Symbol	$RLX.X
Description	BIG LOTS INC		
Pattern	XRV	General Merchandise Stores	

Position	Long	Resistance 2	40.23
Entry	39.24	Resistance 1	39.66
Stop	38.96	Pivot	38.57
Initial Target	39.72	Support 1	38.00
Ratio	1.71	Support 2	36.91
50% To Target	39.48		

BIG PLAN

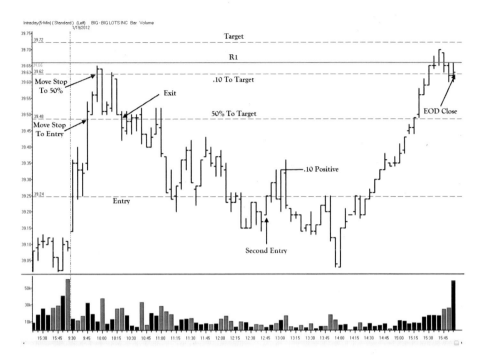

FIGURE A.7 – BIG LOTS
RealTick by Townsend Analytics, Ltd.

I am always excited when Big Lots (BIG) appears on my trading plan. Trading the stock by the rules always seems to pay off and today was no exception. The entry trigger was in the first five minutes of trading. When BIG traveled 50% of the distance from the entry to the target, we moved our stop to break-even. Then, when it moved to the .10 to target level, we moved the trailing stop to the 50% mark. BIG reversed, just shy of R1, and triggered an exit at $39.48.

BIG triggered a second entry at 12:45 ET and made a .10 move in our favour prior to moving .10 against us. This caused us to use the full stop out as the current trail on the position. After reversing lower, BIG moved higher, hit the 50% level, the .10 level, traveled through the R1 pivot and nearly touched the profit target. Another reversal had us exiting the position three minutes before the closing bell at $39.62. The total gain for the day in BIG was $0.62 per share.

Around The Horn Plan
Thursday, January 19, 2012

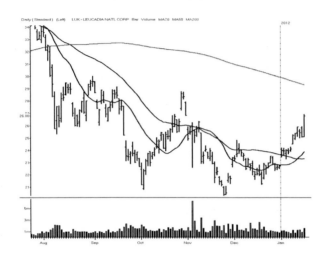

Symbol	LUK	Sector Symbol	$BIX.X
Description	LEUCADIA NATL CORP		
Pattern	XRV	Multi-Sector Holdings	

Position	Long	Resistance 2	28.12
Entry	27.04	Resistance 1	27.46
Stop	26.71	Pivot	26.28
Initial Target	27.57	Support 1	25.62
Ratio	1.61	Support 2	24.44
50% To Target	27.31		

LUK PLAN

FIGURE A.8 – LEUCADIA NATIONAL CORP
RealTick by Townsend Analytics, Ltd.

Leucadia National Corp (LUK) triggered two entries on Thursday. Both traveled 50% to the target, reversed and stopped out at break-even. The stock closed positive on the day, but I never regret following the rules. I am convinced that the strict adherence to the rules over the years has been what kept us in business.

Around The Horn Plan
Friday, January 20, 2012

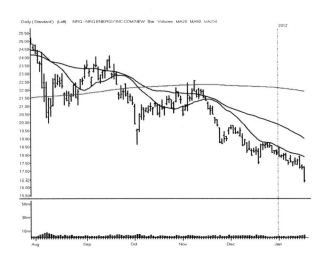

Symbol	NRG	Sector Symbol	$UTY.X
Description	NRG ENERGY INC COM NEW		
Pattern	XRV	Independent Power Producers & Energy Traders	

Position	Short	Resistance 2	17.65
Entry	16.22	Resistance 1	17.03
Stop	16.48	Pivot	16.68
Initial Target	15.83	Support 1	16.06
Ratio	1.50	Support 2	15.71
50% To Target	16.03		

NRG PLAN

FIGURE A.9 – NRG ENERGY INC
RealTick by Townsend Analytics, Ltd.

NRG Energy Inc (NRG) did everything right on Thursday, and I was convinced that follow-through was in the cards for Friday's trading. Unfortunately, after what looked to be a textbook entry, the stock had very little momentum and closed out the session with only $0.07 per share in gains.

Around The Horn Plan
Wednesday, January 25, 2012

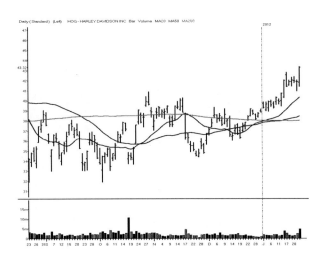

Symbol	HOG		Sector Symbol	$IXY.X
Description	HARLEY DAVIDSON INC			
Pattern	XRV		Motorcycle Manufacturers	

Position	Long	Resistance 2		44.70
Entry	43.50	Resistance 1		44.01
Stop	43.15	Pivot		42.71
Initial Target	44.01	Support 1		42.02
Ratio	1.46	Support 2		40.72
50% To Target	43.76			

HOG PLAN

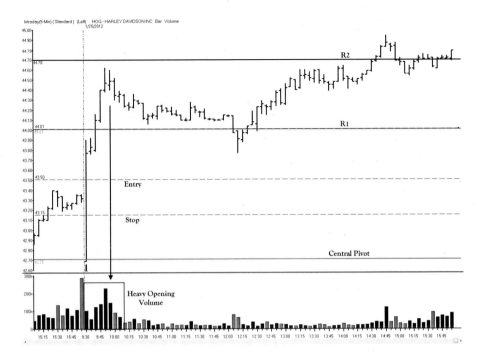

FIGURE A.10 – HARLEY DAVIDSON INC
RealTick by Townsend Analytics, Ltd.

I would guess that Harley Davidson Inc (HOG) appears on my trading more than any other stock. It is a member of the volatile consumer discretionary group, and sets up a pattern entry at least once a month. I like trading HOG, as the intraday moves are fast and predictable, and I have come to know the personality of the stock over the years.

HOG opened for trading at the central pivot, giving us an opportunity for a $42.80 early entry (1). I will take entries like this, as long as they are in the direction of the planned trade, with a stop just below the pivot whenever the opportunity presents itself. In just two minutes, the stock reached the planned entry price and started moving toward the R1 pivot, which also happened to be the target for the position. I always watch trading behaviour around pivot lines, as the amount of price elasticity exhibited there can really provide a great deal of insight into the probability of a profit extension. In the case of HOG, the $44.01 target and R1 overlap were not much of a hurdle, as volume was accelerating with price, and the five-minute close was $.15 above the line. At this point I trailed my stop at R1 - .10 to give the trade a little room to breathe. HOG attempted an extension to the R2 pivot, but fell short. Volume began decreasing, and a reversal of two closes triggered an exit at $44.30.

Around The Horn Plan
Wednesday, January 25, 2012

Symbol	UHS	Sector Symbol	$HCX.X
Description	UNIVERSAL HLTH SVCS INC CL B		
Pattern	XRV	Health Care Facilities	

Position	Long	Resistance 2	42.65
Entry	40.69	Resistance 1	41.55
Stop	40.32	Pivot	39.48
Initial Target	41.09	Support 1	38.38
Ratio	1.08	Support 2	36.31
50% To Target	40.89		

UHS PLAN

FIGURE A.11 – UNIVERSAL HEALTH SERVICES INC
RealTick by Townsend Analytics, Ltd.

Universal Health Services Inc (UHS) was a frustrating trade today as it opened, immediately triggered (1), moved 50% of the distance to the target and stopped out at break-even. All of this happened in the first ten minutes of the session. In the final minutes of the first half hour, UHS triggered another entry (2), and this one resulted in a .10 scratch stop. UHS was not done yet, however, as another entry triggered us in (4) and managed a move to the profit target.

Around The Horn Plan
Thursday, January 26, 2012

Symbol	MTH	Sector Symbol	$HGX.X
Description	MERITAGE HOMES CORP		
Pattern	XRV	Homebuilding	

Position	Long	Resistance 2	29.03
Entry	28.04	Resistance 1	28.39
Stop	27.73	Pivot	27.30
Initial Target	28.40	Support 1	26.66
Ratio	1.16	Support 2	25.57
50% To Target	28.22		

MTG PLAN

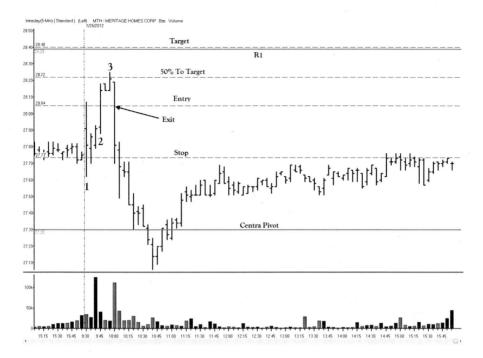

FIGURE A.12 – MERITAGE HOMES
RealTick by Townsend Analytics, Ltd.

Meritage Homes (MTG) opened for trading this morning and immediately generated an entry and a stop out. A few minutes later, a second entry triggered. The result this time was a trip to the 50% mark (3) and back to the entry level for a flat exit. A few minutes later, the stock moved lower to the stop level on its way to the central pivot and lower. MTH was mirroring the activity in the housing sector index, and the index was performing poorly on the session.

APPENDIX B.
Tools of the Trade

I enjoy teaching other traders about what I have learned over the years. I speak at live conferences around the world and on internet webinars many times a year. I make note of what questions people have asked. Although there are sometimes technical questions about one pattern or another, a surprising number of traders ask about computer equipment, brokers, and software. So I thought adding a section to this book to cover my workstation, and what I think is necessary to trade for a living, would be useful to my readers.

THE WAR ROOM

This picture shows the 'War Room'. My wife Julie and I trade here. Even in the context of a husband-and-wife trading team, there is plenty of diversity in what is deemed essential equipment. This is our ideal set-up, and represents a situation in which screen size and quantity are not constrained.

Starting from the left side of the photo, there are horizontal 21-inch monitors. I have three of these, and they are devoted to position management. Each of the position management screens has a daily chart, a five-minute chart, a minder window with a list of correlated securities, a market maker (Level 2 or Total View) window with order entry, and a NYSE OpenBook window.

The two central monitors are 26-inch screens. The bottom one is used to monitor my watch list. The top one scrolls a set of intraday scans so that I can spot opportunities as they evolve. It also monitors charts of all the indices that my trading candidates correlate to. The 30-inch monitor is used to monitor all my set-ups intraday. I have a chart for every trading candidate. Every chart is marked with the entry, stop, initial target and 50%-to-target levels. This makes it very easy for me to assess what is happening across a wide group of symbols over the course of the trading day. I also keep a laptop on the desk during the session to monitor the news wires, as I like to limit my trading computer to running just my trading software.

The small keyboard is a macro-driven order entry device. If I click on a stock chart, all I need to do is press a button on the device and I can get filled in specified lot sizes with predetermined levels of slippage and order staging. I can also use it to modify existing orders and to jockey orders around the inside bid/ask so that I am not left behind in a fast market.

This workstation is what I consider to be the ideal. It gets me in front of all the information that affects my decision-making, and I do not have to change layouts over the course of the session to find the data I am looking for. But that is not to say that everything pictured here is needed to be a profitable trader. Traders have space constraints, and even I frequently trade from other locations using just my laptop.

When I trade from just one monitor, the layout that I use is very different, but still keeps all the relevant decision-making tools where I can find them. In a single monitor configuration, I keep a minder list with all of my trading candidates on screen at all times. Each has an alert set for entry, stop, target, and 50%-to-target, and is linked to a five-minute chart. I keep one large and two small intraday charts on screen, along with a NYSE OpenBook and a Market Maker window with order entry. That is all the information I can make sense of on one screen, and still manage to trade profitably.

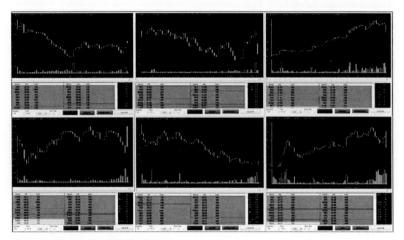

MY MONITOR CONFIGURATION

You can find great *Trade Secrets*
trading set-ups every day at
TraderInsight.com

Every evening, I post stock trading set-ups at **www.traderinsight.com**. At the same
site you can listen to my nightly audio commentary and read my daily watchlist to help
you with the next day's trading. These stocks are the very same ones that I will be
looking to trade. Go to the site today, and be sure to sign up for my free newsletter. I'll
email you new trading ideas, set-ups and actionable market information.

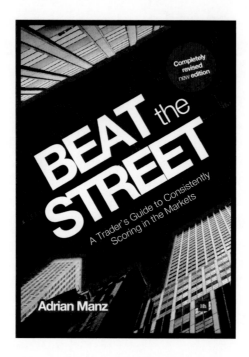